At Issue

What Is the Future of the US Economy?

Other Books in the At Issue Series:

At Issue

What Is the Future of the US Economy?

Ronald D. Lankford, Jr., Book Editor

GREENHAVEN PRESS

A part of Gale, Cengage Learning

GALE
CENGAGE Learning·

Detroit • New York • San Francisco • New Haven, Conn • Waterville, Maine • London

GALE
CENGAGE Learning·

Elizabeth Des Chenes, *Director, Publishing Solutions*

For more information, contact:
Greenhaven Press
27500 Drake Rd.
Farmington Hills, MI 48331-3535
Or you can visit our Internet site at gale.cengage.com

For product information and technology assistance, contact us at

Gale Customer Support, 1-800-877-4253
For permission to use material from this text or product, submit all requests online at www.cengage.com/permissions.

Further permissions questions can be e-mailed to permissionrequest@cengage.com.

Articles in Greenhaven Press anthologies are often edited for length to meet page requirements. In addition, original titles of these works are changed to clearly present the main thesis and to explicitly indicate the author's opinion. Every effort is made to ensure that Greenhaven Press accurately reflects the original intent of the authors. Every effort has been made to trace the owners of copyrighted material.

LIBRARY OF CONGRESS CATALOGING-IN-PUBLICATION DATA

What is the future of the US economy? / Ronald D. Lankford, book editor.
    p. cm. -- (At issue)
  Includes bibliographical references and index.
  ISBN 978-0-7377-6213-6 (hardcover) -- ISBN 978-0-7377-6214-3 (pbk.)
  1. United States--Economic policy--2009- 2. Economic forecasting--United States.
  3. United States--Economic policy--2009- I. Lankford, Ronald D., 1962-
    HC106.84.W47 2012
    330.973001'12--dc23

                                        2012023324

Printed in the United States of America
1 2 3 4 5   16 15 14 13 12

Contents

Introduction

When an economic recession began in the United States in 2007–08, commentators were quick to offer reasons for the financial crisis. Many blamed the US housing and mortgage industry for offering loans that allowed families to purchase homes they could not afford, by requiring little or no down payment and offering initial low monthly payments. Over time, however, the payments increased, leaving many homeowners unable to keep up and eventually going into default on their loans. A number of commentators blamed Wall Street financial companies and banks for careless marketing practices, causing stock market volatility and over-extended loans. Still others blamed the federal government for either too much or too little regulation of the financial market and mortgage industry.

Despite their different roles in the housing meltdown and financial crisis, all of these entities had one thing in common: they were US institutions. Because of this commonality, it was easy to believe that the current economic problems—with the right bailout plan, the right regulations, and the right enforcement of rules—could be fixed. They were problems created in the United States and problems that could likewise be resolved by the country's business leaders and politicians.

By 2009, however, this view—that the United States could fix the recession—proved too narrow. A number of problems relating to the recession, in fact, had their origins in the Middle East, Asia, and Europe. The severe downturn that began in 2007–08 revealed how intricately the United States was connected to economies and markets around the world, and that it could not act unilaterally to fix its ailing economy, despite its status as an economic superpower.

In a very basic way, these connections had always existed: because the United States sold goods around the world, it de-

pended on the economic well-being of other countries to purchase those goods. A recession in one part of the world—as in
Japan during the late 1990s—always had the potential to impact the US economy. Traditionally, however, US manufacturing and service industries had been able to exert a great deal
of control over their economic growth and development, allowing for a measure of independence. More recently, however, the relationship between the United States and other
economies has grown more complicated.

One of the primary factors that strained the US economy
at the end of 2007 was the price of oil. Because the United
States imports nearly 60 percent of its oil supply, the availability of that oil is dependent on many factors that are difficult
to control. Oil shortages, beginning during the 1970s, have led
to higher prices per gallon of gasoline. Likewise, instability in
the Middle East and other oil producing countries has led to
higher prices.

In 2008, the price of gas climbed from $3 to $4 dollars per
gallon; likewise, in the spring of 2012, prices rose to over $4
per gallon in some parts of the country. "At some point, you'll
have a negative feedback loop," stated economist Ed Yardeni.
"High energy prices will correct themselves and if they go
high enough, the negative effects will spill over to stocks and
the economy."[1] No matter how well the economy is managed,
then, the price of gas has the potential to create havoc on
markets and economic growth.

Another factor was the growing economic competition
from countries outside the United States. While there has been
a great deal of discussion about the growing importance of
China and India as economic powers, the problem of economic competition—like the price of oil—dates back to the
1970s. Many European and Asian countries had been devas-
tated by World War II (1939–1945), leaving them unable to
compete in the international market for nearly three decades.
By the 1970s, however, Germany, Japan, and other countries

had re-established themselves as economic powers, allowing them to compete with the United States.

Within the last several years, however, the growing importance of China has impacted US manufacturing and industry. As Americans have increasingly relied on China and other Asian countries for manufactured goods, the country's manufacturing sector has shrunk. US companies have also relied on outsourcing, the practice of paying companies outside the country to manufacture goods that had once been made in America. "China's size, infrastructure and talent pool all indicate a promising future for outsourcing over the coming decade," wrote Egidio Zarella in *Forbes*. "The numbers speak for themselves: in 2009, industry revenues totaled $13 billion and they are projected to grow to $44 billion by 2014...."[2] The growth of manufacturing and industry in China has ultimately equaled fewer high-paying manufacturing jobs in America; most of these jobs have been lost forever and have been replaced with lower-paying service-sector work, which has led to stagnation in US wages. This in turn has contributed to the continued weakness of the US economy.

Over time, the US economy has also become financially entangled in the economies of many other countries. This connection is most clear when American banks loan foreign governments and private industries money. If these governments and industries prosper, they can pay the loans back with interest; if they fail to prosper, experiencing a recession or depression, they may be unable to repay the loans.

Because of this connection, there has been increasing concern within the US banking industry that the economic crisis in Europe will negatively impact US banks (and in turn, the US economy). Specifically, within the European Union there has been a great deal of pressure on countries like Greece, Spain, and Italy to cut government budgets in order to repay loans. "As these events unfold," noted J.D. Foster of the Heritage Foundation, "the essential consequence for the United

States economy is a large dose of bad uncertainty. Bad uncertainty is analogous to bad cholesterol. It builds up and creates economic blockages. In the economic sphere, this shows up as decisions delayed or downscaled, decisions that under normal times would produce the actions that produce growth. Europe is clearly adding to the headwinds facing the economy today."[3]

Outside influences on the US economy can no longer be treated with indifference. Whether one considers the price of oil and potential instability in the Middle East, outsourcing to China and other Asian countries, or the interconnectivity of US and European banking, many economic factors remain beyond the control of US government and business. These factors also greatly complicate gaining an accurate picture of the future of the US economy. These influences do make clear, however, that the United States will increasingly have to consider the impact of oil imports, the outsourcing of manufacturing, and international bank loans when making economic policy.

Notes

1. Jeff Sommer, "Numbers That Sway Markets and Voters," *The New York Times*, March 3, 2012.
2. Egidio Zarella, "China's Competetive Edge in the Outsourcing Space," *Forbes*, October 7, 2010.
3. J.D. Foster, "The European Financial and Economic Crisis: Origins, Taxonomy, and Implications for the U.S. Economy," The Heritage Foundation, September 23, 2011. www .heritage.org.

1

The US Has the Capacity for a Better Economic Future

Thomas L. Friedman and Michael Mandelbaum

Thomas L. Friedman is a foreign-affairs columnist for The New York Times *and Michael Mandelbaum is a professor of American foreign policy at Johns Hopkins University.*

While there is no denying that the United States faces many economic problems today, Americans have always proven strongest when facing adversity. Unfortunately, there are many current economic problems that the political establishment has been unwilling to address. Investing in education, for instance, will be essential in preparing the American workforce for the future. Likewise, the world will continue to need American ingenuity and know-how to prosper. If the United States meets its current challenges as it has met those in the past, America will continue to lead the world toward a bright economic future.

Is America still exceptional? The question has become a contentious issue in American politics over the last few years. But the answer has implications that go well beyond the political fortunes of Republicans and Democrats in the United States. It affects the stability and prosperity of the entire world.

President Barack Obama's Republican critics now routinely accuse him of denying America's history as an "exceptional" country because, when asked about the concept in 2009, he replied, "I believe in American exceptionalism, just as

I suspect that the Brits believe in British exceptionalism and the Greeks believe in Greek exceptionalism." (He then went on to list some of the features that, in his view, make America exceptional.) In [presidential hopeful] Mitt Romney's recent retelling, this is akin to saying that "there is nothing unique about the United States."

Declaring that America is exceptional—that is, exceptionally wealthy, powerful, and dynamic—doesn't make it so.

But the idea of American exceptionalism does have real intellectual grounding. As used by scholars, it refers to the ways the United States has differed historically from the older countries of Europe: the fact that it was founded on a set of ideas; that it lacked a hierarchical social order with a hereditary aristocracy at the top; that the Europeans who settled North America did so in a huge, sparsely populated territory; and that it attracted immigrants from all over the world. In American politics, the term has come to have a celebratory as well as an analytical meaning. It refers to what makes America special: its wealth, its power, the economic opportunity it has provided for its citizens, and the expansive role it has played in the world, including the example of liberty and prosperity that it has set.

Accessing American Exceptionalism

The fuss over exceptionalism represents, in one sense, politics as usual in the United States, with one side accusing the other of being out of touch with the country's deepest values: a "profoundly mistaken view," Romney said of Obama's "derisive" remarks. It also, however, taps into the national current of unease about the country and its future, an unease that is, alas, all too justified. No American politician will publicly question his or her country's exceptional status, but it is worth asking whether America really is still exceptional, especially because so many Americans are beginning to worry privately—and some publicly—that it is not.

The question reminds us of a story attributed to Abraham Lincoln. He asked, "If you call a horse's tail a leg, how many legs does a horse have?" He then responded, "The answer is four, because calling a horse's tail a leg doesn't make it one." Similarly, declaring that America is exceptional—that is, exceptionally wealthy, powerful, and dynamic—doesn't make it so. Exceptionalism is not a distinction that is bestowed and then lasts forever, like an honorary degree from a university; nor is it an entitlement like Social Security or Medicare—something all Americans automatically get to enjoy at a certain age. It has to be earned continually, like a baseball player's batting average. And today, as so many Americans fear, it is not being earned. America's exceptionalism is now in play. To remain exceptional, America must respond effectively to its four great 21st-century challenges: the ones posed by globalization, the revolution in information technology, the country's huge and growing deficits, and its pattern of energy consumption. America does not now have in place the policies needed to master them.

The global governance the United States has provided . . . has rested on a vibrant economy and the national unity and confidence that have arisen from it.

The United States has not adapted its educational system to prepare Americans for well-paying jobs in a world economy shaped by globalization and the revolution in information technology. It has not mustered the political will to bring the deficits of its federal government and many of its state and local governments under control. It has not taken effective steps to jump-start the long transition away from heavy reliance on fossil fuels.

Underlying these specific failures is a national failure even to pose the questions that must be answered as the starting point for all public policies: What world are we living in, and what do we need to do to thrive in it?

United States and Global Economics

The stakes are exceptionally high. For Americans, whether the United States is able to answer these questions successfully will determine the country's future rate of economic growth, and that growth rate will in turn determine how much Americans will be able to maintain the best features of their society: opportunity, mobility, and social harmony. For the rest of the world, the stakes are perhaps even higher. Since 1945, and especially since the end of the Cold War, the United States has provided to the world many of the services that governments generally furnish to the societies they govern. While maintaining the world's major currency, the dollar, it has served as a market for the exports that have fueled remarkable economic growth in Asia and elsewhere. America's Navy safeguards the sea lanes along which much of the world's trade passes, and its military deployments in Europe and East Asia underwrite security in those regions. The U.S. military also guarantees the world's access to the oil of the Persian Gulf, and American intelligence assets, diplomatic muscle, and occasionally military force resist the most dangerous trend in contemporary international politics: the proliferation of nuclear weapons. The global governance the United States has provided, from which the rest of the world has derived enormous benefit, has rested on a vibrant economy and the national unity and confidence that have arisen from it.

In 2011, a robust American global role continues to be vital. With the Arab world in upheaval; with Europe's common currency, the euro, in crisis and the future of the European Union itself in doubt; and with China, the world's fastest-growing economy and fastest-rising power, having all but exhausted the possibilities of its model for economic growth based on an undervalued currency and ever-rising exports, a dynamic American economy and a stabilizing, reassuring American global presence are as important now as they have ever been, if not more so. Sustaining them, though, depends on America's rising to meet its major challenges, and doing so immediately.

If one were to design a country ideally suited to flourish in the 21st century, it would look more like the United States than any other.

Somehow it has fallen slightly out of fashion to talk about "American power." Those on the left often do not fully understand its constructive uses, concentrating instead on the occasional abuses that always attend the exercise of power. Those on the right often do not fully understand its sources—that American power is not simply a matter of will but of means, and those means need to be constantly renewed and refreshed. In the second decade of the 21st century, that depends on successfully meeting the country's four major domestic challenges.

Can America respond to them in appropriate fashion? We are optimistic that it can. While the country is paralyzed at the top—the political system is stuck and is not generating the necessary public policies—it remains extraordinarily vibrant at the grassroots.

If one were to design a country ideally suited to flourish in the 21st century, it would look more like the United States than any other. In a world in which individual creativity is becoming ever more important, America supports individual achievement and celebrates the quirky. In a world in which technological change takes place at warp speed, requiring maximal economic flexibility, the American economy is as flexible as any on the planet. In a world in which transparent, reliable institutions, and especially the rule of law, are more important than ever for risk-taking and innovation, the United States has an outstanding legal environment. In a world in which even the cleverest inventors and entrepreneurs have to try and fail before succeeding, American business culture understands that failure is often the necessary condition for success. None of these traits has gone away during the current crisis.

Meeting Future Challenges

Over the course of its history, the United States has rarely failed to meet its major challenges. It is in fact the current failure to do so that is unusual—one might even say "exceptional." When tested, from the days of the revolution in the 18th century to the drawn-out Cold War struggle in the 20th, America and Americans have found ways to excel.

The United States has greater potential than any other country to thrive in the future by becoming the world's most attractive launching pad.

To continue to do so, the country would do well to learn from the experience of one of its iconic companies, IBM, which is celebrating its centennial this year. IBM essentially invented the personal computer, but didn't fully understand the implications of its own creation. The company, like too many Americans, came to think of its exceptional status as self-perpetuating and permanent. This led to complacency and strategic mistakes that almost proved fatal.

How did IBM lose sight of the world it invented? Listen carefully to the answer of Samuel Palmisano, IBM's current chairman and CEO, when we asked him that question: "You spend more time arguing amongst yourselves over a shrinking pie than looking to the future," he said, and so "you miss the big turn" that you have entered, even a turn that your own company invented. When you mistakenly start thinking of other departments and colleagues in your own company as the opposition—rather than the other companies against which you must compete—you have lost touch with the world in which you are operating. This can be as lethal for countries as it is for companies. America's political parties today have strayed off course, Palmisano told us, "because they have focused on themselves" more than on the priorities of the country as a whole. IBM got back on track, under new leadership, by focusing on and coming to understand the new environment in which it was operating and then mobilizing and inspiring the whole company to master the next big change in technology, networked computing.

America needs to do something similar. It is obvious what its core competency is in the 21st century. The United States has greater potential than any other country to thrive in the future by becoming the world's most attractive launching pad—the place where everyone wants to come to work, invent, collaborate, or start something up to get the most out of our new hyperconnected world. And they will want to come to America because it has the best infrastructure, the most dynamic schools, the most open economy, the most inviting immigration policies, the most efficient and stable markets, the most government-funded research, and the best rules to promote risk-taking and prevent recklessness. That is how America remains as "exceptional" in this century as it was in the last two—not by launching another moon shot but by becoming the world's favorite launching pad for millions of moon shots.

American power and prosperity, and global stability and prosperity, are all riding on the country's success in meeting its challenges. A world influenced by a United States powerful enough to provide political, economic, and moral leadership will not be a perfect world, but it will be a better world than any alternative we can envision. That means that the status of

American exceptionalism is more than an academic controversy or a partisan political squabble in the United States. Everyone, everywhere, has an interest in America taking the steps necessary to remain an exceptional country.

2

The US Is Undergoing a Depression

Jason Kirby

Jason Kirby is a senior writer at Mclean's.

The current US economic crisis has been misunderstood, partly because it has been misnamed: the recession, in reality, is a depression. At the base of this new depression lies a massive job crisis: millions of Americans are either unemployed or underemployed. Even more troubling, it appears that the current slump in available jobs began before the 2007 "recession." Unless the government is willing to heavily invest in a public jobs' program and education, it is unclear when the economic situation will improve.

Everywhere Darren Enns looks these days he sees the devastation wrought by America's grinding employment crisis. As the treasurer of a construction union in southern Nevada, the state with the highest unemployment in the country, Enns has watched as friends and colleagues—the bricklayers, electricians and drywallers who thrived during Las Vegas's housing boom—struggle to move on to other careers. Few succeed. Many have simply given up hope. "When you look at the unemployment rate during the Great Depression, we're beyond that in the construction industry here in Las Vegas," he says. "We've got close to 70 per cent unemployment, so for us, the economy is extremely depressed."

Jason Kirby, "The Dreaded D-Word: Is America's Current Economic Crisis Part of a Whole New Great Depression That Actually Began in 2007?" *Maclean's*, vol. 124, no. 37, September 26, 2011. p. 33. Copyright © 2011 by Maclean's. All rights reserved. Reproduced by permission.

When the financial crisis tipped America into a deep recession in 2007, it was tempting to draw comparisons to the Great Depression of the 1930s. Those fears subsided once the stock market pulled out of its nosedive and America's economy began to grow again, albeit at a crawl. It was a brief respite. Four years later, American towns and cities remain overrun with millions of unemployed workers even as the economy risks slipping back into reverse. It raises the question whether the U.S. ever really emerged from recession in the first place. Instead, some are suggesting those early fears may have been justified after all: the United States appears to be in the throes of an outright jobs depression.

What to call the current crisis has always been a difficult task because there is no set definition for what constitutes a depression.

An Extended Economic Crisis

Earlier this month, Robert Reich, a professor of public policy at Berkeley and the secretary of labour in the [Bill] Clinton administration, said the current crisis is an extension of the "depression" that began in December 2007. Meanwhile, Richard Posner, a high-profile judge in the United States Seventh Circuit Court of Appeals and regular political and economic commentator, said it's time for America to give up any false hopes that the economy is on a path to recovery. "If we were being honest with ourselves, we would call this a depression," he wrote in the *New Republic*. "That would certainly better convey both the severity of our problems, and the fact that those problems have no evident solutions."

What to call the current crisis has always been a difficult task because there is no set definition for what constitutes a depression. The National Bureau of Economic Research in Washington is the organization tasked with identifying the official start and end of recessions—loosely defined as two or more consecutive quarters of negative growth—but it steers clear of identifying depressions. That's partly because depressions are as rare as they are terrible. Yet there are similarities to what is happening now, and what America went through in the decade after 1929.

Most people don't realize the Great Depression was in fact two separate recessions that history blended into one long malaise. The first and deepest recession lasted from 1929 to 1933 and was followed by a period of slow but positive economic growth. Then in 1937 the U.S. tipped back into recession for another 13 months. Many economists have warned that the U.S. is at risk of a double-dip recession, similar to what happened in the 1980s, when a brief recession in 1980 was quickly followed by another downturn from 1981 to 1982. If America's economy does shrink for a second time this decade, though, the gap between the two recessions would bear more likeness to the calamity of the 1930s.

The employment situation is arguably far worse than the official unemployment rate shows.

To be clear, the downturn that occurred in 2007 was neither as deep or as devastating as the recessions of the 1930s, when the economy shrank by a staggering 25 per cent. (The recession in 2009 involved a correction of just four per cent.) But there are other worrying parallels, and they have to do with the brutal state of America's job market.

The Job Market

The World Got a sense of how grim the situation is when the latest job numbers for August [2011] were released, showing the country created zero net jobs. The unemployment rate remained unchanged at 9.1 per cent, roughly where it has been stuck since mid-2009. Most worrisome of all, as Reich, the

Berkeley professor, pointed out, as of August America's total available labour force has expanded by seven million people since the start of the recession in 2007 thanks to population growth, yet the number of working Americans has actually shrunk by 300,000.

Across the nation scenes of desperation are playing out each day. When a baby food company in Fresno, Calif., held a job fair to fill 40 openings last week, 600 job seekers turned out with resumes. In New York, troubled Bank of America confirmed it would axe 30,000 jobs, though it has yet to say how many pink slips will go out to workers in the U.S. versus overseas.

The employment situation is arguably far worse than the official unemployment rate shows. That's because it doesn't include those workers who have simply given up looking for work, or those who have settled for part-time jobs. When those individuals are factored in, the true unemployment picture jumps to 16.2 per cent, which is unnervingly closer to the 21 per cent peak reached in 1934.

Buried within the ugly jobs data is an even uglier reality— the crisis in America's job market began long before the current recession, and it could be years before it ends. It's well known that men have been particularly hard hit by the jobs crisis, but only now are economists realizing how bad the situation is. For one thing, only 63.5 per cent of men have any type of job whatsoever, full- or part-time, which is the lowest level since records began in 1948, according to Bloomberg. Worse still, with so many men shut out of work, incomes have been pushed down to levels not seen in decades. In a recent report, the Hamilton Project at the Brookings Institution found real wages for men have fallen 28 per cent since 1969. For men without a high school degree, real wages plunged 66 per cent.

Economists can't agree on what's behind the malaise. Some argue high unemployment is the result of low demand brought on by the recession, so the answer is more government stimulus. Others point to structural changes in the job market, such as the eradication of low-skilled jobs through automation and globalization, that have left workers ill-prepared for what employers need. Surprisingly, in some parts of the country companies are screaming for workers, despite the glut of job hunters. As of July there were 3.2 million job openings in the U.S., with companies in the tech sector and even plastics manufacturing struggling to fill positions.

This crisis has all the hallmarks of an outright depression, whether anyone wants to call it that or not.

Long-Term Economic Investments

Alan Berube, a research director with the Brookings Institution, says persistent high unemployment is the result of both weak demand and deeper shifts in the economy. In a new study, Berube and his colleague Jonathan Rothwell examined the education gap in 366 U.S. metropolitan areas, meaning the difference between the years of schooling needed for the average local job and the years of schooling job seekers actually have. They found that cities with a wider gap experienced higher unemployment levels than those without. "This gap is not a new phenomenon, the recession just put a point on it" says Berube. The housing bubble masked the deeper problems in the economy by providing an abundance of temporary low-skilled jobs in the construction industry. "When that mask was peeled away after the housing crisis hit, that education gap and the impacts of it were revealed once again." The solution, he says, is to boost the number of people completing post-secondary educations and to retrain workers. Both tasks will be difficult at a time when governments are under pressure to slash spending.

Critics charge President Barack Obama's jobs plan, which would direct $100 billion to infrastructure projects, is just more of the same and doesn't fix long-term problems. Instead of building houses, workers would build schools, but they'll still be unsuited for the economy of the future after the stimulus money dries up.

Berube disagrees. "The needs are great, the question is, does the nation have the willingness to invest in things that we're going to need for long-run economic growth," he says. "If we need these [infrastructure investments] then I don't think it's masking a problem, it's taking advantage of the skills that are already there."

Amid the uncertainty and political wrangling in Washington, one thing is certain—for the long-term unemployed, this crisis has all the hallmarks of an outright depression, whether anyone wants to call it that or not.

3

The Future of the US Economy Is Mixed

Martin Neil Baily

Martin Neil Baily served as an advisor on the Council of Economic Advisors during the Bill Clinton administration. He is currently a senior fellow at the Brookings Institution.

While there are a number of indicators that the US economy is improving, these signs must be balanced against several potential problems, from the availability of oil to the ongoing economic crisis in Europe. Even as the US economy has improved since the initial recession of 2007–08, growth has been slow. Many businesses have been hesitant to make new investments, and the housing sector continues to struggle. The United States may be on the verge of an economic recovery, but if the economic crisis in Europe deepens, the American recovery seems less likely.

The recovery in the United States has remained sluggish because there are too many anchors weighing it down. The continued weakness in the housing market has kept residential construction at depression levels. Historically, U.S. recoveries have always featured a lift from housing, this has not happened in this recovery and it may be another couple of years before all of the foreclosures are worked through. The good news is that residential construction has stopped falling, but housing prices are still declining slowly on average. The housing problems are not spread evenly around the country but rather are concentrated in five states, California, Nevada, New Mexico, Florida and Michigan. This raises the hope that there may be a gradual pickup in housing prices and home construction in other regions even though the excess supply of housing still persists in these five states. Policy efforts to mitigate the ongoing tide of foreclosures have had only a very modest impact and it seems that only time will heal this wound.

One endogenous [caused by factors inside the system] response to the housing crisis has been that fewer new households have been formed as people choose to live with parents or share housing with others. Another response has been a sharp increase in the demand for rental housing, which has in turn triggered construction of multifamily units. The housing recovery will be skewed to multifamily, which is better than nothing but such units have a much lower cost per unit than single family houses and hence contribute less to overall demand.

There is a widespread view that businesses in the U.S. are holding back on investment and hiring because they are afraid of the huge budget deficits.

The weakness in the housing market has contributed to the loss of household wealth. The stock market has recovered much of the huge drop it took in the financial crisis as corporate profits have been strong, but the volatility of markets has made it hard for consumers to take a lot of comfort from the partial recovery of financial wealth. The consumer deleveraging process continues as debt levels are reduced and borrowing remains subdued. Much of the reduction in household debt so far has come about through defaults and foreclosures rather than repaying debts.

Beyond housing, the other big anchor weighing down the economy is the weakness in household income that is driven primarily by the weakness in the labor market. In fact over the past several quarters, consumer spending has grown a little faster than disposable income, so the saving rate has declined slightly. Consumers are certainly cautious, but *the big reason consumer spending growth is slow is that income growth is slow or negative.*

A Slow-Growth Economy

There is a widespread view that businesses in the U.S. are holding back on investment and hiring because they are afraid of the huge budget deficits and their potential to cause a new financial crisis or because they think their taxes will go up a lot. There are additional concerns around the costs imposed by new health care and financial regulation as well as a fear that some version of cap and trade will be introduced and raise energy costs. Assessments of this viewpoint are divided politically, with liberals like Paul Krugman dismissing the idea and focusing instead on demand weakness. However, there is no question that businesses are holding a lot of cash on their balance sheets; indeed the Federal Reserve reports that the cash share of corporate assets is at its highest level since 1959. My own judgment is that by far the biggest reason for weak hiring is the lack of strong demand growth. But rather than seeing this issue as either-or, it is better to view the two views as reinforcing each other. Companies are hesitant to invest and hire mostly for demand reasons, reinforced by regulation and deficit concerns.

It is noteworthy that business investment is actually picking up quite well for both non residential structures and equipment and software. Hiring is indeed still sluggish, so much of the investment so far seems to be replacement investment (including the replacement cycle for IT [information technology] equipment) or cost-saving rather than for expansion. And the level of business investment is still lower than it was prior to the recession.

The other pieces that go into aggregate demand include government purchases, net exports, and inventories. Of these three, government purchases are declining now because of cutbacks by states and localities, and this decline in government demand may well continue into the future as federal purchases are cut back also, given the strong emphasis in Washington on cutting the deficit. Clearly there is a need for fiscal restraint here but if federal spending is cut quickly, this will have a short term negative impact on demand, something that is being demonstrated in the European setting. Net exports have been helping the U.S. economy for a couple of quarters or so as exports rise faster than imports but the overall impact is small and will likely dissipate in a weakening global economy. Inventories are pretty much impossible to forecast and often have a big impact on the GDP [Gross Domestic Product] for a given quarter. As long as U.S. production continues at a reasonable pace, inventory accumulation will help that growth, but if growth were to weaken an inventory cycle could easily be the catalyst for a double dip.

Turmoil in the mideast is bad news for U.S. and global growth.

Positive Signs of an Economic Recovery

Despite these problems, the mood on the economy has improved in the past couple of months with many forecasters starting to revise up their forecasts instead of constantly revising them down. This is not true everywhere—the Federal Reserve and OECD [Organization for Economic Co-Operation and Development] cut their 2012 U.S. forecasts, but these institutions are catching up to the bad economic data in the first half of this year more than responding to the improvement in recent months. Few are expecting really strong growth any time soon, but the chances of a double dip have diminished. GDP growth averaging 2 to 3 percent for the next few quarters seems quite likely and growth in excess of 3 percent is possible in 2012. (Strong export numbers and inventory accumulation could push growth in the fourth quarter above 3 percent).

There are risks to this forecast, of course, with Europe being the main one, but first I will mention two other risks, political deadlock and oil prices. Coming out of the debt ceiling agreement, the special Joint Congressional (Super) committee was charged with finding $1.5 trillion or more of budget cuts (over the 10 year budget window) and they were not able to reach an agreement. Democrats insisted on tax increases on upper income households and the Republicans resisted. The provision of the debt ceiling agreement was that in the event of a committee failure, there are automatic federal expenditure cuts of $1.2 trillion triggered in the form of across the board reductions (with some exceptions). The cuts would be equally split between defense and non defense and would exempt Social Security and low-income programs. Medicare cuts would be limited to 2%. On the face of it you might think this would be a popular outcome for Republicans who are pushing for spending cuts, but that is not the case because of the defense cuts, which would come on top of restraints on the military budget already agreed to. (As part of the debt ceiling agreement, Obama already imposed caps on discretionary spending that are worth $750 billion over 10 years ($900 billion including interest saving)).

The across-the-board spending cuts would start in January 2013. These cuts would not be huge in terms of the annual budget, but across the board cuts are not a good solution and they would be a damper on demand. Now that the "Super Committee" has failed there will likely be an effort to modify the automatic cuts in a way that spares the defense budget. The failure of the super committee has actually left Obama with some negotiating power. He has said he would veto any bill that voided the defense cuts but did not represent a broad deficit reduction effort on the grounds that Congress "needs to do its job" in coming up with the full quota of budget cuts (which in practice means agreeing to tax increases on upper income taxpayers). Of course, we may end up with another frustrating and destabilizing cliffhanger like the debt limit and, if so, the resulting uncertainty will harm the recovery.

Other Potential Recovery Problems

Concerns about Iran have pushed the price of oil to around $100 a barrel and a new spike in oil prices would pose a substantial risk to the recovery. I do not know how to assess the risks here in terms of Iran. Turmoil in the mideast is bad news for U.S. and global growth.

The prospects for the U.S. recovery . . . are mixed.

Turing to Europe: There was agreement at the recent EU [European Union] leaders meeting to impose much stricter fiscal controls over members, with only Britain saying no. In return, the leaders agreed to beef up the bail-out fund for countries that get into trouble rolling over their debt obligations. Although [Prime Minister of Germany Angela] Merkel and other leaders rejected the idea of a Eurobond that would impose formal joint liability on all countries for the debts of any single country, a larger bail-out fund may effectively achieve the same result. A coordinated approach to the debt problem is attractive because there is enough economic strength in the region as a whole to support the level of region-wide sovereign debt at a favorable rate of interest. As long as they are protected under the umbrella of the stronger economies, the governments of Italy, Spain and other weaker economies should be able to service their own debt payments. Any debt guaranty from Germany and the stronger economies would only have to be activated if economic conditions were to deteriorate going forward. Given the resistance of the electorates of the strong economies to taking on the risk of having to bail out one or more of the weaker economies, however, the euro debt crisis is not over yet.

Moreover, the agreement reached by the EU leaders has its own pitfalls. The strict budget rules will dampen aggregate demand in Europe and make it more likely that the region will end up in a serious recession, a recession that could even worsen budget deficits. Austerity measures are a two-edged sword. And the role of the European Central Bank is not yet clear. The ECB could play an important role in stabilizing the sovereign debt market through its ability to buy sovereign bonds. And it has played this role at times. However, ECB head Mario Draghi has also made it clear that he expects the EU governments to solve the debt problem themselves and not rely on the ECB as a possible lender of last resort to sovereign governments.

The pessimistic outcome in Europe is the case where the big plan fails and individual countries try to muddle through. In that case, there is a significant danger that financial institutions that have sovereign debt on their books will be liquidity constrained because no one wants to lend to them (this is already a problem). Their own governments could be unable to borrow additional funds to keep the institutions from failing. A cascading series of institutional failures would endanger the whole European financial system.

The prospects for the U.S. recovery, therefore, are mixed. There are continuing problems in the housing market and the vicious circle of low income and low consumer spending continues to keep the economy down. There are signs, however, that the recovery is beginning to take hold and the vicious cycle could turn into a more virtuous cycle of rising income, declining unemployment and stronger demand. The intrinsics of the U.S. economy are good enough to suggest a more sustainable recovery is possible, even likely, in 2012. The biggest danger to the recovery is from a serious setback in Europe. The second biggest is from political conflict here at home.

4

The US Population Is Increasingly Divided By Wealth

Patrick Martin

Patrick Martin is a writer for the World Socialist Web Site, an online publication that opposes the capitalist market system and seeks to establish socialism throughout the world.

As the American economy has deteriorated, the division between the super-rich and the poor has grown dramatically. As the job crisis has grown worse, many American children (one in four) have had to depend on food stamps to "get by." Meanwhile, other Americans possess excessive wealth, allowing them to buy influence in Congress.

America at Christmas 2011 is a society of mass poverty, on the one hand, and vast wealth accumulation, on the other—tens of millions of people are poor and desperate, while a relative handful enjoy riches undreamt of by the Egyptian pharaohs or the aristocracy of Louis XIV.

Government agencies and social service groups document the tidal wave of human need in statistics that are increasingly mind-boggling: 50 million Americans live below the official poverty line, while another 100 million live in "near-poverty," struggling to support themselves on incomes so low that they are one misfortune away from destitution.

The Job Crisis

Some 25 million workers are either unemployed or underemployed, 50 million live without health insurance, one out of every seven Americans receives food stamps. The number of self-employed Americans has fallen by two million over the past five years. Nearly six million of the jobless have been out of work for more than six months.

The jobs crisis has steadily worsened, not only year-to-year, but decade after decade. American capitalism continues to generate record corporate profits and wealth for the super-rich, but is less and less able to provide employment for working people.

One out of every four American children depends on food stamps. Some 1.6 million children were homeless at some point or other during this year [2011].

According to a study by the McKinsey consulting firm, it took six months for the US economy to return to pre-recession job levels after the 1982 recession. After the 1991 recession, the recovery in jobs required 15 months. After the 2001 recession, it took 39 months.

Some 48 months have already passed since the current slump in the labor market began, and there are six million fewer people employed than in December 2007. McKinsey initially forecast that it would take 60 months before jobs regained the level of 2007, but at the current level of job creation, it would take 78 months to reach the level of 146 million workers employed before the onset of the recession—assuming that there is no further deepening of the economic slump.

The protracted duration of mass unemployment is the driving force of a social crisis that blights the future of young and old. One out of every four American children depends on food stamps. Some 1.6 million children were homeless at some point or other during this year. For young workers aged 18 to 24, jobless rates exceed the Depression level of 20 percent. Nearly 20 percent of all American men between the ages of 25 and 34 are now living with their parents.

The Dwindling American Dream

Meanwhile, those nearer the end of their working life have little to look forward to: according to the Employee Benefit Research Institute, 46 percent of all American workers have less than $10,000 saved for retirement, and 29 percent of all American workers have less than $1,000 saved for retirement.

While the vast majority of the American people confront increasing difficulty in meeting their basic social and economic requirements, the financial aristocracy lives in a different universe.

Four million American families have seen their homes foreclosed since the subprime mortgage crisis first erupted in 2007. Nearly 12 million families occupy homes that are under water, financially speaking—the mortgage debt is more than the dwellings are worth in the depressed housing market.

The entire political establishment, the Obama White House and Congress alike, is callously indifferent to the suffering of the population. The Democrats and Republicans speak for different wings of the same ruling elite.

While the vast majority of the American people confront increasing difficulty in meeting their basic social and economic requirements, the financial aristocracy lives in a different universe. One recent example sheds considerable light.

The New Aristocracy

As the *New York Times* reported this week, one charter member of this aristocracy, former Citigroup chairman Sandy Weill, has just sold his penthouse apartment in Manhattan for $88 million. The purchaser was 22-year-old Ekaterina Rybolovleva, daughter of Russian oligarch Dmitriy Rybolovlev, the monopoly owner of the former Soviet fertilizer industry.

The squandering of such a vast sum to house a single individual naturally provokes outrage and revulsion. The $88 million expended for the penthouse at 15 Central Park West is greater than the entire annual operating deficit of the Metropolitan Transportation Authority ($68 million), or the 2010 annual budget deficit of the city of Detroit ($58 million). It approximates the cost of all free school lunches in the New York City schools for an entire school year.

By a straightforward calculation, $88 million would provide 2,000 jobs for unemployed workers at the average US wage of $44,000 a year. While Mr. Weill and Ms. Rybolovleva are among the "job creators" celebrated by American politicians, Democrats and Republicans, who oppose raising taxes on the super-rich, neither of them provided employment on that scale. And if anything, the demeaning employment of chauffeurs, doormen, maids and security men who serve the whims of such billionaires constitutes a drain on society, not a benefit.

Buying Politicians

There is another yardstick for measuring this waste of social resources. Sandy Weill is best known as the wheeler-dealer who combined his Travelers insurance empire with Citibank, creating Citigroup as the first and largest of the financial supermarkets, companies able to throw their weight around in every area of financial services.

In 1998–99, Weill launched an all-out lobbying campaign to sway the Republican-controlled Congress and the Democratic White House to support repeal of the Glass-Steagall Act, the Depression-era law, passed in the wake of the 1929 Wall Street crash, that made illegal the type of financial octopus created by Weill.

Weill bought Congress and the [Bill] Clinton administration for $100 million, not much more than the price at which he sold his Manhattan penthouse last month.

5

Forgiving Student Loans Will Improve the US Economy

Robert Applebaum

Robert Applebaum is a lawyer in Staten Island, New York, and the founder of ForgiveStudentLoanDebt.com, an advocacy group and website devoted to helping current and former students struggling with excessive amounts of student loan debt.

Student debt—perhaps as high as one trillion dollars—is responsible for holding back many American workers. Furthermore, this debt is putting an additional strain on the US economy. After finishing a higher education degree, many students have accumulated the kind of debt associated with a mortgage loan. Because of this debt, these typically young workers are unable to contribute to the economy by buying homes, raising children, and going on vacations. By forgiving that debt, the government will unleash the purchasing power of these workers, who will then be in a better position to contribute to a US economic recovery.

A week ago, President Barack Obama unveiled a series of executive orders to address the ever-growing student loan debt crisis in America. Billed by the White House as a direct response to a petition I created on the White House's new "We the People" petition site, the president announced the implementation of already-passed changes to the government's student loan program.

The changes could be found in the fine print. The Income Based Repayment (IBR) program included in last year's Affordable Care Act would be moved up from 2014 to 2012. And certain types of federal loans would be eligible for consolidation and enrollment in IBR. That was it. That was the entirety of the president's response to a petition signed by over 30,000 Americans calling for across-the-board student loan forgiveness as a means of economic stimulus. Obama also announced the creation of a new form that would allow people to calculate their educational costs and repayment obligations. Inspirational? Hardly.

Here's the problem: there's only so much the president can do on his own without a Congress willing to do the job it was elected to do. So while I was disappointed by just how little the president's new initiative would help the vast majority of Americans drowning in student loan debt, I was encouraged by the fact that he at least acknowledged the problem: a $1 trillion student loan debt overhang that isn't going away any time soon.

In fact, it's growing larger by the day, and its effects are felt by everyone. President Obama's inability to adequately address the concerns raised by those who signed the We the People petition (not to mention the over *651,000 people* who've signed the same basic petition I created on MoveOn.org's new petition site, SignOn.org) highlights the limits of unilateral executive power. The president can be criticized for being tone-deaf to the needs of the people, but I think that criticism is more appropriately reserved for the do-nothing 112th Congress. But I digress.

Forgiveness as Stimulus

The movement to forgive student loan debt as a means of economic stimulus started out by accident, prompted by an essay I wrote in January 2009 as I was watching cable news coverage of the debate over the proposed "Obama Stimulus

Plan." A mere nine days after the inauguration of a man ushered into office on a platform of "hope and change," yet, there we were, having the same tired old debate over tax cuts, corporate welfare and the demonstrably failed ideology of trickle-down economics.

As someone who has student loan debt myself, it occurred to me that if I were suddenly relieved of my obligation to repay the approximately $500 in student loan payments that I dutifully make each and every month without fail, I'd have an extra $500 per month, *every month*, to spend on ailing sectors of the economy. Think of it as a trickle-up approach to economic stimulus.

My point in writing the essay wasn't to say that I didn't want to pay back what I had borrowed. Rather, it was to say that if we truly wanted to stimulate economic growth, I had a better, more efficient way of accomplishing that goal.

The president's new "Pay as You Earn" initiative is unlikely to help very many people for several reasons.

Generally speaking, the whole purpose of obtaining a higher education is to get further ahead in life; to better contribute to society.

First, the IBR repayment plan is available only to those with federal loans. Those drowning in private student loan debt, which often carries usurious interest rates and exceedingly few good options for anyone experiencing any sort of trouble repaying their loans, are ineligible.

Second, one of the requirements for eligibility for IBR is that you must be current on your repayments. Those who aren't current on their repayments, almost by definition, need the additional help now, arguably even more than those who are current. Asking them to repay thousands of dollars on their student loans *before* they can even apply for this "help" is like a hospital telling a gunshot wound victim that he has to remove the bullet himself, before the hospital will consider whether to stop the bleeding.

Saddling Students with Debt

Contrary to what the regressive right would have you believe, the calls for student loan forgiveness are not about a generation of self-entitled, pot-smoking, lazy deadbeats looking for a handout. It's about restoring some semblance of sanity to the student lending industry that has made a mockery of the very objective behind obtaining a higher education in the first place.

Generally speaking, the whole purpose of obtaining a higher education is to get further ahead in life; to better contribute to society; to be successful and to share the spoils of that success with the next generation. If we're routinely failing to accomplish any of those goals, and if millions of Americans are graduating into much worse financial positions than they otherwise would have been in had they never chosen to go to school at all, then what is the point of seeking out a higher education at all?

Sadly, from the perspective of the student loan industry, the point is to rake in hundreds of billions of dollars by preying upon the youngest, least financially savvy and most economically vulnerable among us by continuing to advance the farce of the so-called American dream that's been slowly but surely slipping away since the 1980s.

Saddling entire generations of current and former students with massive educational debt comes with huge opportunity costs. As a result, the "educated poor" are not buying homes, not starting businesses or families, not inventing, investing or innovating and otherwise engaging in economically productive activities we need all Americans to be doing right now if we're ever to dig ourselves out of the hole created by the greed of those at the top.

And, let me be clear about who the "educated poor" really are. Yes, some of them are recent college grads and 20-somethings, but just as many are in their 30s, 40s, 50s and beyond—people who have paid for their educations several times over but who still have balances in the tens of thousands of dollars.

With so much seemingly free money flooding the system in the form of student loans, anyone with a pulse and a desire to obtain a higher education degree can avail themselves of a loan.

Don't believe me? Check out the new website, Occupy StudentDebt.com, that my organization, ForgiveStudentLoan Debt.com, is undertaking with the folks behind the film *Default: The Student Loan Documentary*. Relieving these taxpaying Americans of their student loan debt obligations would usher in an era of broad-based entrepreneurship, innovation and prosperity.

Unfortunately, the top 1 percent and their cheerleaders on the right would rather focus on how "unfair" such a proposal is, as if the situation *their* policies have created is in any way "fair" to the millions of Americans holding student loan debts. Their narrow-minded, ill-informed reactions can be summed up with a familiar phrase: "I got mine, Jack, so screw you!"

The Heart of the Problem

Student loans themselves are the problem. A well-intentioned program designed to give access to higher education to those who could otherwise not afford one has had the (unintended?) consequence of turning education into a commodity with highly disturbing parallels to the subprime mortgage mess. With so much seemingly free money flooding the system in the form of student loans, anyone with a pulse and a desire to obtain a higher education can avail themselves of a loan. As tuition rates have soared, the very same degrees that now cost nearly five times the amount they did a just a few decades ago are worth significantly less in today's decimated job market.

The sad but undeniable truth is that, through student loans, we've shifted all of the burdens not only of obtaining an education but of maintaining a bloated educational system *down* the socioeconomic ladder on those who can least afford to shoulder the costs.

Then, once they graduate, we expect them to repay hundreds and, oftentimes, thousands of dollars per month in student loan repayments, despite approximately five applicants for every job opening and despite the fact that middle-class wages have gone down, not up, over the last 10 years.

Is it any wonder that so many people find themselves in financial trouble, causing a downward spiral of debt from which there is almost no escape? Student loans have been stripped of nearly all basic consumer protections such as bankruptcy and statutes of limitations, thereby eliminating any risk on the part of the lenders in issuing these loans.

If a student loan borrower misses a payment, fees of up to 25 percent of the principal can be tacked on to the bottom line and, if the loan should go into collections, up to another 25 percent of the principal can be tacked on in penalties, all of which gets capitalized, meaning that the principal balance grows exponentially, eliminating any and all hope, short of winning the lottery or robbing a bank, that these debts can ever be repaid.

What Can Be Done?

So, where does all of this leave us? With Occupy protests spreading to every major city all across the country, clamoring for student loan forgiveness (among other demands), hundreds of thousands of people energized and mobilized for a long, hard fight. One member of Congress, Rep. Hansen Clarke, D-Mich, has even introduced a House resolution calling on Congress to endorse the idea of reducing home mortgage balances and student loan debt.

We need a Congress willing to work with the president on easing the enormous burdens faced by millions of Americans who find themselves in such dire straits because they made the decision to better themselves through higher education.

There's a whole host of things that Congress and the president can and should do right away. I continue to think across-the-board student loan forgiveness will provide a sustained economic stimulus for the next 20-30 years, and reaffirm that an education is something actually worth pursuing.

No other industrialized country in the world treats education and the financing thereof the way we do here in America.

But short of that there is no good reason why anyone should be able to have his or her gambling debts discharged or restructured in bankruptcy, but not their student loans.

There is no good reason why the collections of student loans shouldn't be subject to statutes of limitations, just as any other cause of action, civil or criminal (other than murder), is subject to.

And there is no good reason why banks and other financial institutions can avail themselves of low- or no-interest government loans while students must borrow at interest rates of 6.8 percent or more just to obtain an education.

No other industrialized country in the world treats education and the financing thereof the way we do here in America and few sane people would argue that *this* is the best we can do. But without a Congress willing to do its job, initiatives such as what the president unveiled last week are pretty much the best we can hope for, which is to say, not a whole lot.

6

Student Loans May Have a Negative Impact on the US Economy

Marcy Gordon

Marcy Gordon is a reporter for the Associated Press.

Once, low-income students were the most likely to rely on college loans. In the 2000s, however, rising tuition costs outstripped the ability of many families to finance higher education for their children. As a result, more loans became available from private institutions. While these loans allowed students to earn a degree, many had high interest rates and significant penalties if borrowers fell behind in payments or defaulted. As such, graduates left college faced with a mountain of debt, even before they began their careers. While this debt has a negative effect on the lifestyles of graduates, it also has the potential to impact the broader US economy. As the economy has grown worse, observers fear that the student loan industry could face the same kind of crisis as the mortgage loan industry faced in 2007 and after.

The near doubling in the cost of a college degree the past decade has produced an explosion in high-priced student loans that could haunt the U.S. economy for years.

While scholarship, grant money and government-backed student loans—whose interest rates are capped—have taken up some of the slack, many families and individual students have turned to private loans, which carry fees and interest rates that are often variable and up to 20%.

Many in the next generation of workers will be so debt-burdened they will have to delay home purchases, limit vacations, even eat out less to pay loans off on time.

Kristin Cole, 30, who graduated from Michigan State University's law school and lives in Grand Rapids, Mich., owes $150,000 in private and government-backed student loans. Her monthly payment of $660, which consumes a quarter of her take-home pay, is scheduled to jump to $800 in a year or so, confronting her with stark financial choices.

"I could never buy a house. I can't travel; I can't do anything," she said. "I feel like a prisoner."

A legal aid worker, Cole said she may need to get a job at a law firm, "doing something that I'm not real dedicated to, just for the sake of being able to live."

Parents are still the primary source of funds for many students, but the dynamics were radically altered in recent years as tuition costs soared and sources of readily available and more costly private financing made higher education seemingly available to anyone willing to sign a loan application.

Rocketing tuition fees made borrowing that much more appealing.

Students with no credit history and no relatives to co-sign loans (or co-signing parents with tarnished credit) were willing to bet that high-priced loans were a trade-off for a shot at the American dream. But high-paying jobs are proving elusive for many graduates.

"This is literally a new form of indenture . . . something that every American parent should be scared of," said Barmak Nassirian, associate executive director of the American Association of Collegiate Registrars and Admissions Officers.

More than $17 billion in private student loans were issued last year, up from $4 billion a year in 2001. Outstanding student borrowing jumped from $38 billion in 1995 to $85 billion last year [2006], according to experts and lawmakers.

Rocketing tuition fees made borrowing that much more appealing. Consumer prices on average rose less than 29% over the past 10 years while tuition, fees, and room and board at four-year public colleges and universities soared 79% to $12,796 a year and 65% to $30,367 a year at private institutions, according to the College Board.

Scholarship and grant money have increased, yet for almost 15 years, the maximum available per person in government-guaranteed student loans, which by law can't charge rates above 6.8%, has remained at $23,000 total for four years. That's less than half the average four-year tuition, room and board of $51,000 at public colleges and $121,000 at private institutions.

Sallie Mae, formally known as SLM Corp., has been on the winning side of the loan bonanza. Its portfolio of 10 million customers includes $25 billion in private and $128 billion in government-backed education loans. However, private-equity investors who had offered $25 billion to buy the company backed out last week, citing credit market weakness and a new law cutting billions of dollars in subsidies to student lenders.

Citigroup Inc., Bank of America Corp., JPMorgan Chase & Co., Wells Fargo & Co., Wachovia Corp. and Regions Financial Corp. are also big players in the private student loan business. And there has been an explosion in specialized student loan lenders, such as EduCap, Nelnet Inc., NextStudent Inc., Student Loan Corp., College Loan Corp., CIT Group Inc. and Education Finance Partners Inc.

The question is whether everyone who borrowed will be able to repay. Experts don't track default rates on private student loans, but many predict sharp increases in years to come.

Dr. Paul-Henry Zottola, a 35-year-old periodontist in Rocky Hill, Conn., faces paying $1,600 a month on his student loan on top of a $2,300 mortgage payment and $1,500 on the loan he took out to start his practice.

His credit record remains solid but he owes more than $300,000 in student loans as he and his wife, Heather, an elementary school administrator, raise two young children.

"It would be very easy to feel crushed by it," Zottola said in an interview. "All my income for the next 10 years is spoken for."

Critics say what happened in the mortgage market could happen in the student loan market.

Meanwhile, complaints about marketing of private loans—like ads promising to approve loans worth $50,000 in just minutes—are on the rise. The complaints have made their way to lawmakers, who see a need to regulate the highly profitable and diverse group of companies and the loans they make to college students.

In August, the Senate Banking Committee approved a bill that would mandate clearer disclosure of rates and terms on private student loans. The bill also would require a 30-day comparison shopping period after loan approval, during which time the offer terms could not be altered.

New York Attorney General Andrew Cuomo said many graduates who borrowed owe as much if not more than most homeowners owe on mortgages. Unlike mortgages with clear consumer disclosure requirements—even from non-bank lenders, private lending is "the Wild West of the student loan industry," he said in a telephone interview.

Critics say what happened in the mortgage market could happen in the student loan market. Cuomo, who conducted a nationwide investigation, said the parallels between the two markets are provocative.

Demand for bundled student loans sold to institutional investors worldwide fueled lending to students. The market for private student loan-backed securities leapt 76% last year [2006], to $16.6 billion, from $9.4 billion in 2005, according to Moody's Investors Service.

[Some] critics allege widespread corrupt arrangements propelled a student loan boom.

The student loan-backed securities market has yet to suffer noticeable effects of a global credit squeeze that was triggered this summer by a mortgage meltdown of borrowers with risky credit.

"Once the economy starts to slow, you're going to see a large increase of these people in bankruptcy court," said Robert Manning, a professor at Rochester Institute of Technology who has written about college students and credit cards.

A 2005 change to bankruptcy law puts private student loans on par with child support and alimony payments: Lenders can garnish wages if someone doesn't pay.

Cuomo's probe revealed what he calls an "appalling pattern of favoritism" for student lenders that provided kickbacks, revenue-sharing plans and trips to college administrators in exchange for recommended lender status. Other critics allege widespread corrupt arrangements propelled a student loan boom.

Lenders deny such charges, arguing that industry growth resulted from surging education costs and that higher interest rates are justified for unsecured loans to borrowers with blemished or insufficient credit records.

"Lenders take 100% of the repayment risk on flexible private-education loans made to people with limited credit histories, on which they will not get repaid for several years," Barry Goulding, a Sallie Mae official, told Congress last spring.

New regulations could dry up access to education financing, he and other industry executives argue. Some experts are skeptical, predicting waves of student loan delinquencies and defaults on what is outstanding.

"Should private student loans suffer the same sort of failure as (subprime) mortgages, as students graduate or drop out and find themselves unable to pay, we will do serious damage not only to the lives of many students but also to the economic and social fabric of our country that depends on college graduates for its strength," said Luke Swarthout at the U.S. Public Interest Research Group.

7

Returning Manufacturing Jobs Will Strengthen US Economy

Brendan I. Koerner

Brendan I. Koerner has worked as a contributing editor for Wired *magazine and as a columnist for* Slate.

Over time, many American manufactures have chosen to move factories to Mexico, China, and other countries, seeking cheaper labor and less regulation. More recently, however, a number of US manufactures are discovering that outsourcing is less profitable than previously thought. As a result, a number of these businesses are relocating in the United States, allowing for local control and better quality. As a result of this shift, manufactures are hiring more Americans, providing jobs for an ailing US economy. While it seems unlikely that the United States will regain its former prominence in manufacturing, the shift to domestic production is a positive sign for the country's economic future.

In early 2010, somewhere high above the northern hemisphere, Mark Krywko decided he'd had enough. The CEO [Chief Executive Officer] of Sleek Audio, a purveyor of high-end earphones, Krywko was flying home to Florida after yet another frustrating visit to Dongguan, China, where a contract factory assembled the majority of his company's prod-

Brendan I. Koerner, "Coming Home: In a Radical Departure, Many Businesses Are Discovering That Manufacturing Their Products Onshore Rather than Abroad Is More Efficient—And Cheaper," *Saturday Evening Post*, vol. 283, no. 5, September/October 2011, p. 56. Copyright © 2011 by Brendan I. Koerner. All rights reserved. Reproduced by permission.

ucts. He and his son, Jason, Sleek Audio's co-founder, made the long trip every few months to troubleshoot quality flaws. Every time the Krywkos visited Dongguan, their Chinese partners assured them everything was under control.

Those promises almost always proved empty.

As he whiled away the airborne hours, Krywko made a mental list of all the manufacturing glitches that had nearly wrecked his company. There was the entire shipment of 10,000 earphones that Sleek Audio had to discard because they were improperly welded, a mistake that cost the company millions. Then there were the delivery delays caused by the factory's lackadaisical approach to deadlines, which forced the Krywkos to spend a fortune air-freighting products to the U.S. Even when orders were produced on schedule, Krywko wasn't too pleased with the situation: The company always had precious cash tied up in inventory that took months to arrive after the prototypes had been approved.

The headaches had finally become too exasperating to bear. And so, on that flight, he turned to Jason and said that he was done with Dongguan. "I can't do it anymore," he said. "Let's bring it home."

For U.S. firms, the decision to manufacture overseas has long seemed a no-brainer.

Jason had been thinking the same thing.

From Offshore to Domestic Manufacturing

When the Krywkos returned to the United States, they searched for a manufacturing partner with the tools and expertise to produce their earphones. They found one just a few miles away from their Palmetto, Florida, headquarters: Dynamic Innovations, a maker of ruggedized computers and other equipment. Sleek Audio quickly signed up.

Today, more than a year since Krywko's decision to go against the offshoring tide, Sleek Audio has a full-scale manufacturing operation that can be reached via a 15-minute car ride rather than a 24-hour flight. Each earphone costs roughly 50 percent more to produce in Florida than in China, but Krywko is more than happy to pay the premium to know that botched orders and shipping delays won't ruin his company. And so far, the gambit appears to be paying off: Based on enthusiastic customer response, Sleek Audio is assured of having its most profitable year ever.

For U.S. firms, the decision to manufacture overseas has long seemed a no-brainer. Labor costs in China and other developing nations have been so cheap that—as recently as two or three years ago—anyone who refused to offshore was viewed as a dinosaur, certain to go extinct as bolder companies built the future in Asia. But stamping out products in Guangdong Province is no longer the bargain it once was, and U.S. manufacturing is no longer as expensive. As the labor equation has balanced out, companies—particularly the small to medium-size businesses that make up the innovative guts of America's technology industry—are taking a long, hard look at the downsides of extending their supply chains to the other side of the planet.

The core component of offshoring, of course, is cheap labor.

"Companies are looking to base their decisions on more than just costs," says Simon Ellis, head of supply-chain strategies practice at IDC Manufacturing Insights, a market research firm. Indeed, when accounting giant KPMG International recently asked 196 senior executives to list their top concerns for 2011 and 2012, labor costs ranked below product quality and fluctuations in shipping rates and currency values. And 25 percent of the companies that responded to a January

2011 survey by MFG.com, an online sourcing marketplace, said they had recently brought all or part of their manufacturing back to North America from overseas, up from 12 percent in the first quarter of 2010. This is one reason U.S. factories managed to add 136,000 jobs last year—the first increase in manufacturing employment since 1997.

The United States certainly isn't on the verge of recapturing its past industrial glory, nor can every business benefit by fleeing China. But those that actually build tangible goods should no longer assume that "Made in the U.S.A." is an unaffordable luxury. Unless a company is hell-bent on selling the cheapest goods possible without regard to quality, manufacturing at home makes more sense than it has in a generation.

[Chinese] factories are so overbooked that they have no choice but to favor their biggest clients. The smaller customers can end up burdened with long delays or hastily assembled products (or both).

Inexpensive Overseas Labor

China's big manufacturing advantage has been cheap labor, but wages—while still low compared with those in the U.S.—have risen sharply in recent years.

Think of offshoring as a technology. Like any relatively young and successful innovation, it enjoyed a honeymoon period during which everyone scrambled to adopt it lest they miss out on the gold rush. But now many companies are starting to grapple with this new technology's limitations.

The core component of offshoring, of course, is cheap labor. In 2000, when Congress was preparing to vote on normalizing trade relations with China, political opponents of the bill gave their colleagues satchels containing three pennies—supposedly the average hourly wage for Chinese workers. That figure was exaggerated, but the spirit of the stunt rang true:

U.S. manufacturers couldn't possibly compete with China's blend of rock-bottom wages and rising technical savvy. After the bill passed, the offshoring trickle that started in the 1980s became an unbridled flood.

Chinese factories deftly took advantage of this situation by making it easy for even the smallest U.S. startups to find manufacturing partners. Factories polished their English-language outreach and established ties with professional middlemen. Soon anyone with a blueprint and modest capital could hire a Chinese factory to stamp out 20,000 units of a video tripod, an ergonomic joystick, or an espresso machine.

But the system has started to overheat. Manufacturing wages more than doubled in China between 2002 and 2008, and the value of the nation's currency (the yuan) has risen steadily. China is now under tremendous international pressure to let the yuan appreciate even more, and the country must cope with worrisome inflation at home (food prices rose by nearly 12 percent last year). And though Chinese workers still earn a fraction of what their American counterparts do, the rising costs of labor there are prompting companies to re-evaluate their production strategies.

Quality Control Issues

After they do, these businesses often realize something profound: China isn't the great deal they expected. A January 2010 survey by the consulting firm Grant Thornton found that 44 percent of responders felt they got no benefit from going overseas while another 7 percent believed that offshoring had actually caused them harm. This problem is due largely to China's success: Factories are so overbooked that they have no choice but to favor their biggest clients. The smaller customers can end up burdened with long delays or hastily assembled products (or both).

"If you're a huge company like Apple, you can get the whole factory to work for you," says Paul King, founder of

Hercules Networks, a New York company that makes charging kiosks for mobile devices. "You can put your own process in place. You can have your own quality control. But without that kind of power, you're just another customer, and they don't really care." King cycled through three Chinese factories from 2008 to 2010 before giving up on offshoring due to persistent manufacturing errors—LCDs [liquid crystal displays] that winked out after six months and lights that broke when tapped even gently. The quality woes have disappeared now that Hercules is making its kiosks in the U.S., King says, and the company is thriving.

When you include all the various drawbacks and costs that don't appear in a factory's price quote, manufacturing certain high-tech goods in China can end up being surprisingly expensive.

To deal with their production backlogs, many Chinese factories have started subcontracting work to facilities located in the center and western areas of the country, where labor costs are cheaper than on the industrialized coasts. But this usually makes the problems even worse. "They'll subcontract your work without providing the subcontractor with the same training that you provided to them," says George T. Haley, a professor of industrial and international marketing at the University of New Haven who specializes in Chinese business. "Then, all of a sudden, your quality assurance goes all to hell."

Other Drawbacks

Beyond the quality issues, subcontracting also exacerbates a second major problem with Chinese manufacturing: the lack of safeguards on intellectual property. The more subcontractors that get their hands on a design, the greater the odds of theft. Peerless Industries, an Illinois company that makes flatscreen and projector mounts, learned that lesson the hard way. "Knockoffs of our products started showing up in markets here in our own backyard," says Michael Campagna, Peerless Industries' chief operating officer. "It wasn't necessarily our supplier doing it—it was our supplier's supplier."

There is a common strategy among businesses that elect to manufacture in the U.S.: Redesign with labor costs in mind.

Finally, sheer distance remains an intractable problem. Shipping costs nose-dived in the wake of the 2008 financial crisis but have since crept up as oil prices once again approach the $100-a-barrel mark. And then there's simply the time it takes to get goods from China. With credit hard to come by these days, companies are reluctant to tie up cash in inventory that takes three to six months to manufacture, ship, and clear customs.

When you include all the various drawbacks and costs that don't appear in a factory's price quote, manufacturing certain high-tech goods in China can end up being surprisingly expensive. In 2008, three McKinsey consultants analyzed the production of midrange servers, taking into account everything from shipping to quality to exchange rates. They concluded that fabricating such devices in China made sense in 2003 when the required labor was 60 percent cheaper there than in the United States. At that time, they estimated, the per-unit savings ran about $64. But this advantage, McKinsey concluded, had vanished by 2008. "After factoring in the higher labor and freight costs, we find that the former offshore savings have turned negative—a burden of an extra $16."

Redesigning Domestic Products

There is a common strategy among businesses that elect to manufacture in the U.S.: Redesign with labor costs in mind. "We've redesigned products five or six times, trying to reduce the number of connectors, the number of screws, anything that would require additional labor," says Albert VanLeeuwen, chief financial officer of QSI Corporation, a Salt Lake City manufacturer of rugged data terminals that has resisted the siren call of Asia. "With some of the products we're introducing this year, we've decreased the labor content 40 percent."

Another way to limit production cost is to swap in less expensive though equally resilient materials. When Hercules Networks' King severed ties with China, he had an engineering firm analyze his charging kiosks. It found that the Chinese factories had been using an unnecessarily heavy metal that could be replaced easily with an aluminum composite. King estimates that this and other design tweaks have enabled him to make his kiosks in the U.S. for barely five percent more per unit than in China—and he thinks that soon there won't be any premium.

Even if a company gets stuck paying a little extra, though, it's often a wise trade-off, especially for companies that need to be nimble enough to make changes on the fly. For example, many businesses look to bigger players to determine the price of parts. If a Goliath decides to order millions of a certain component, the Davids can benefit by incorporating the suddenly cheap widget into their products as well—but only if they do it quickly, while loads of that part are being made. Executing such rapid changes is difficult when the factory is 8,000 miles away.

Large companies don't only determine parts for their smaller brethren; they also create demand for innovative products that complement their own. (Think, for instance, of the enormous accessories industry that's sprung up to support mobile phones and audio players.) The best way for companies to capitalize on new demand generated by something like the iPad is to act quickly, getting their wireless keyboard or speaker system on the market before the competition. When time is of the essence, there are obvious advantages to having a supply chain that's thousands of miles shorter than your rivals'.

"Our sales team had a meeting in October and found out there was no articulating wall mount available for the Samsung 9000 TV," says Campagna of Peerless Industries, which is now manufacturing in Aurora, Illinois. "Within four weeks, we'd designed a new mount and had it on the market. No way could we have done that in China. It probably would have taken us eight to 12 weeks."

To be sure, the age of offshoring is far from over.

True, Peerless probably could have made those mounts in China for a bit less. But the company would have entered a market already flooded with competitors instead of leading the way.

New Manufacturing Trends

A company that sells tens of thousands of units a year may no longer see the wisdom of sending its manufacturing to China. But what if that company wants to scale up and sell millions? Big customers get more than just the best price quotes and most prompt service from Asian factories; they also frequently receive massive government subsidies and perks. When a nation offers to pay hundreds of salaries and throw in free land to boot, an ambitious company can find it hard to say no.

But there is evidence that large corporations are no longer automatically swayed by these goodies. In October 2009, NCR decided to stop manufacturing its North American-market ATMs [automated teller machines] at facilities in China and India and make them instead in Columbus, Georgia. Last October, General Electric elected to invest $432 million in four new U.S. manufacturing facilities that will build environmentally friendly refrigerators and water heaters. These are precisely the sort of companies that stand to benefit the most by heading overseas. But they determined that the smarter long-term play was to narrow the physical distance between R&D [research & development] and production. "By colocating all the people who are involved in bringing a product to life, we increase collaboration and problem-solving and shorten development time," says Kevin Nolan, GE Appliances' vice president of technology.

To be sure, the age of offshoring is far from over. The largest companies will continue to manufacture overseas more often than not—the raw economics still demand it. After a company gets big enough, it can afford to hire full-time staff in Asia or build its own factories outside Shenzhen, taking advantage of cheap labor without incurring many of the headaches that haunt smaller players.

But, for many companies, distance will continue to matter for one simple reason: In a supply chain, the tighter the connection between each point, the lower the risk of something going haywire. That risk can be tolerated when the benefits of stretching the connections are too great to ignore. But when those benefits diminish, it's time to consider building a system that is stable by design. And once America's formidable innovation muscle is focused on keeping manufacturing nearby, new and inventive systems will be developed quickly.

After all, it's one thing to gamble on a new design, but it's quite another to entrust your company's fortunes to the whims of a Dongguan factory owner.

8

The US Job Market Is Increasingly Unfavorable for the Middle Class

Andy Kroll

Andy Kroll is a reporter in the Washington, D.C. bureau of Mother Jones.

During the recent economic downturn, Americans have been increasingly forced to take low-paying jobs and part-time work, leading to a long-term shift in the US job market. Like the economy as a whole, this new balance will serve to increase wages for those with higher education and the right skills while decreasing wages for the unskilled. Likewise, those in the center—the traditional middle class—will continue to lose ground. These trends have been supported by the decreasing influence of big labor, a traditional ally of the working middle class. Even public sector unions—for firefighters, police, and teachers—have come under assault as state budgets have dwindled. Whether these downward trends continue remains an open question.

Think of it as a parable for these grim economic times. On April 19th [2011], McDonald's launched its first-ever national hiring day, signing up 62,000 new workers at stores throughout the country. For some context, that's more jobs created by one company in a single day than the net job creation of the entire U.S. economy in 2009. And if that boggles the mind, consider how many workers applied to local

McDonald's franchises that day and left empty-handed: 938,000 of them. With a 6.2% acceptance rate in its spring hiring blitz, McDonald's was more selective than the Princeton, Stanford, or Yale University admission offices.

It shouldn't be surprising that a million souls flocked to McDonald's hoping for a steady paycheck, when nearly 14 million Americans are out of work and nearly a million more are too discouraged even to look for a job. At this point, it apparently made no difference to them that the fast-food industry pays some of the lowest wages around: on average, $8.89 an hour, or barely half the $15.95 hourly average across all American industries.

Yes, jobs are being created, but what kinds of jobs paying what kinds of wages?

On an annual basis, the average fast-food worker takes home $20,800, less than half the national average of $43,400. McDonald's appears to pay even worse, at least with its newest hires. In the press release for its national hiring day, the multibillion-dollar company said it would spend $518 million on the newest round of hires, or $8,354 a head. Hence the Oxford English Dictionary's definition of "McJob" as "a low-paying job that requires little skill and provides little opportunity for advancement."

Of course, if you read only the headlines, you might think that the jobs picture was improving. The economy added 1.3 million private-sector jobs between February 2010 and January 2011, and the headline unemployment rate edged downward, from 9.8% to 8.8%, between November of last year and March. It inched upward in April, to 9%, but tempering that increase was the news that the economy added 244,000 jobs last month (not including those 62,000 McJobs), beating economists' expectations.

Under this somewhat sunnier news, however, runs a far darker undercurrent. Yes, jobs are being created, but what kinds of jobs paying what kinds of wages? Can those jobs sustain a modest lifestyle and pay the bills? Or are we living through a McJobs recovery?

The Rise of the McWorker

The evidence points to the latter. According to a recent analysis by the National Employment Law Project (NELP), the biggest growth in private-sector job creation in the past year occurred in positions in the low-wage retail, administrative, and food service sectors of the economy. While 23% of the jobs lost in the Great Recession that followed the economic meltdown of 2008 were "low-wage" (those paying $9–$13 an hour), 49% of new jobs added in the sluggish "recovery" are in those same low-wage industries. On the other end of the spectrum, 40% of the jobs lost paid high wages ($19–$31 an hour), while a mere 14% of new jobs pay similarly high wages.

As many labor economists have begun to point out, we're witnessing an increasing polarization of the U.S. economy over the past three decades.

As a point of comparison, that's much worse than in the recession of 2001 after the high-tech bubble burst. Then, higher wage jobs made up almost a third of all new jobs in the first year after the crisis.

The hardest hit industries in terms of employment now are finance, manufacturing, and especially construction, which was decimated when the housing bubble burst in 2007 and has yet to recover. Meanwhile, NELP found that hiring for temporary administrative and waste-management jobs, healthcare jobs, and of course those fast-food restaurants has surged.

Indeed in 2010, one in four jobs added by private employers was a temporary job, which usually provides workers with few benefits and even less job security. It's not surprising that employers would first rely on temporary hires as they regained their footing after a colossal financial crisis. But this time around, companies have taken on temp workers in far greater numbers than after previous downturns. Where 26% of hires in 2010 were temporary, the figure was 11% after the early-1990s recession and only 7% after the downturn of 2001.

Job Polarization

As many labor economists have begun to point out, we're witnessing an increasing polarization of the U.S. economy over the past three decades. More and more, we're seeing labor growth largely at opposite ends of the skills-and-wages spectrum—among, that is, the best and the worst kinds of jobs.

At one end of job growth, you have increasing numbers of people flipping burgers, answering telephones, engaged in child care, mopping hallways, and in other low-wage lines of work. At the other end, you have increasing numbers of engineers, doctors, lawyers, and people in high-wage "creative" careers. What's disappearing is the middle, the decent-paying jobs that helped expand the American middle class in the mid-twentieth century and that, if the present lopsided recovery is any indication, are now going the way of typewriters and landline telephones.

Because the shape of the workforce increasingly looks fat on both ends and thin in the middle, economists have begun to speak of "the barbell effect," which for those clinging to a middle-class existence in bad times means a nightmare life. For one thing, the shape of the workforce now hinders America's once vaunted upward mobility. It's the downhill slope that's largely available these days.

The barbell effect has also created staggering levels of income inequality of a sort not known since the decades before the Great Depression. From 1979 to 2007, for the middle class, average household income (after taxes) nudged upward from $44,100 to $55,300; by contrast, for the top 1%, average household income soared from $346,600 in 1979 to nearly $1.3 million in 2007. That is, super-rich families saw their earnings increase 11 times faster than middle-class families.

The Role of Technology and Education

What's causing this polarization? An obvious culprit is technology. As MIT economist David Autor notes, the tasks of "organizing, storing, retrieving, and manipulating information" that humans once performed are now computerized. And when computers can't handle more basic clerical work, employers ship those jobs overseas where labor is cheaper and benefits nonexistent.

In a recent Gallup poll, a majority of people agreed that the country was still in either a depression (29%) or a recession (26%).

Another factor is education. In today's barbell economy, degrees and diplomas have never mattered more, which means that those with just a high school education increasingly find themselves locked into the low-wage end of the labor market with little hope for better. Worse yet, the pay gap between the well-educated and not-so-educated continues to widen: in 1979, the hourly wage of a typical college graduate was 1.5 times higher than that of a typical high-school graduate; by 2009, it was almost two times higher.

Considering, then, that the percentage of men ages 25 to 34 who have gone to college is actually decreasing, it's not surprising that wage inequality has gotten worse in the U.S. As Autor writes, advanced economies like ours "depend on their best-educated workers to develop and commercialize the innovative ideas that drive economic growth."

The distorting effects of the barbell economy aren't lost on ordinary Americans. In a recent Gallup poll, a majority of people agreed that the country was still in either a depression (29%) or a recession (26%). When sorted out by income, however, those making $75,000 or more a year are, not surprisingly, most likely to believe the economy is in neither a recession nor a depression, but growing. After all, they're the ones most likely to have benefited from a soaring stock market and the return to profitability of both corporate America and Wall Street. In Gallup's middle-income group, by contrast, 55% of respondents claim the economy is in trouble. They're still waiting for their recovery to arrive.

The Slow Fade of Big Labor

The big-picture economic changes described by Autor and others, however, don't tell the entire story. There's a significant political component to the hollowing out of the American labor force and the impoverishment of the middle class: the slow fade of organized labor. Since the 1950s, the clout of unions in the public and private sectors has waned, their membership has dwindled, and their political influence has weakened considerably. Long gone are the days when powerful union bosses—the AFL-CIO's George Meany or the UAW's Walter Reuther—had the ear of just about any president.

As *Mother Jones'* Kevin Drum has written, in the 1960s and 1970s a rift developed between big labor and the Democratic Party. Unions recoiled in disgust at what they perceived to be the "motley collection of shaggy kids, newly assertive women, and goo-goo academics" who had begun to supplant organized labor in the Party. In 1972, the influential AFL-CIO symbolically distanced itself from the Democrats by refusing to endorse their nominee for president, George McGovern.

All the while, big business was mobilizing, banding together to form massive advocacy groups such as the Business Roundtable and shaping the staid U.S. Chamber of Commerce into a ferocious lobbying machine. In the 1980s and 1990s, the Democratic Party drifted rightward and toward an increasingly powerful and financially focused business community, creating the Democratic Leadership Council, an olive branch of sorts to corporate America. "It's not that the working class [had] abandoned Democrats," Drum wrote. "It's just the opposite: The Democratic Party [had] largely abandoned the working class."

An Assault on Workers' Rights

The GOP, of course, has a long history of battling organized labor, and nowhere has that been clearer than in the party's recent assault on workers' rights. Swept in by a tide of Republican support in 2010, new GOP majorities in state legislatures from Wisconsin to Tennessee to New Hampshire have introduced bills meant to roll back decades' worth of collective bargaining rights for public-sector unions, the last bastion of organized labor still standing (somewhat) strong.

> *At precisely the moment when middle-class workers need strong bargaining rights so they can fight to preserve a living wage . . . unions around the country face the grim prospect of losing those rights.*

The political calculus behind the war on public-sector unions is obvious: kneecap them and you knock out a major pillar of support for the Democratic Party. In the 2010 midterm elections, the American Federation of State, County, and Municipal Employees (AFSCME) spent nearly $90 million on TV ads, phone banking, mailings, and other support for Democratic candidates. The anti-union legislation being pushed by Republicans would inflict serious damage on AFSCME and other public-sector unions by making it harder for them to retain members and weakening their clout at the bargaining table.

And as shown by the latest state to join the anti-union fray, it's not just Republicans chipping away at workers' rights anymore. In Massachusetts, a staunchly liberal state, the Democratic-led State Assembly recently voted to curb collective bargaining rights on heath-care benefits for teachers, fire-fighters, and a host of other public-sector employees.

Bargaining-table clout is crucial for unions, since it directly affects the wages their members take home every month. According to data from the Bureau of Labor Statistics, union workers pocket on average $200 more per week than their non-union counterparts, a 28% percent difference. The benefits of union representation are even greater for women and people of color: women in unions make 34% more than their non-unionized counterparts, and Latino workers nearly 51% more.

In other words, at precisely the moment when middle-class workers need strong bargaining rights so they can fight to preserve a living wage in a barbell economy, unions around the country face the grim prospect of losing those rights.

All of which raises the questions: Is there any way to revive the American middle class and reshape income distribution in our barbell nation? Or will this warped recovery of ours pave the way for an even more warped McEconomy, with the have-nots at one end, the have-it-alls at the other end, and increasingly less of us in between?

9

China Threatens
US Economic Dominance

Arvind Subramanian

Arvind Subramanian is a senior fellow at the Peterson Institute.

While American political leaders have noted China's economic rise, they have nonetheless failed to assess its true threat to markets in the United States. Because observers have used inaccurate methods to calculate the difference between the Chinese and American economies, the threat has seemed less immediate. When considering other factors such as the standard of living, however, it becomes obvious that the Chinese economy will quickly outpace that of America. If the United States wishes to compete in the global market, it will have to reckon with the increasing influence of China on the world's economy.

The world's two economic superpowers will meet soon for the third installment of their Strategic and Economic Dialogue. Beyond the specifics, the real issue for the United States and the world is China's looming economic dominance. President Obama's State of the Union address, after President Hu Jintao's visit in January [2011], showed the level of anxiety that policymakers feel about China as a potential rival and perhaps a threat, with growing economic, military and political power, including its bankrolling of American debt. But judging from the reaction to the president's speech, that threat is not viewed as imminent. The same was said, some pointed out, of the rise of Russia and Japan, 40 and 20 years ago, respectively, and those threats turned out to be false alarms.

But what if the threat is actually greater than policymakers suppose?

It has long been recognized that using the market exchange rate to value goods and services is misleading about the real costs of living in different countries.

According to the International Monetary Fund, for example, total U.S. gross domestic product in 2010 was $14.7 trillion, more than twice China's $5.8 trillion, making the average American about 11 times more affluent than the average Chinese. Goldman Sachs does not forecast the Chinese economy overtaking that of the United States until 2025 at the earliest. Americans also draw satisfaction from their unmatched strengths of an open society, an entrepreneurial culture, and world-class universities and research institutions.

Assessing China's Threat

But these beliefs may be overly sanguine. The underlying numbers that contribute to them are a little misleading because they are based on converting the value of goods and services around the world into dollars at market exchange rates.

It has long been recognized that using the market exchange rate to value goods and services is misleading about the real costs of living in different countries. Several goods and services that are not traded across borders (medical care, retail services, construction, etc.) are cheaper in poorer countries because labor is abundant. Using the market exchange rate to compare living standards across countries understates the benefits that citizens in poor countries enjoy from having access to these goods and services. Estimates of purchasing power parity take account of these differing costs and are an alternative, and for some purposes a better, way of computing and comparing standards of living and economic output across countries.

The economic advantage China is gaining will only widen in the future.

My calculations ... show that the Chinese economy in 2010, adjusted for purchasing power, was worth about $14.8 trillion, surpassing that of the United States. And, on this basis, the average American is "only" four times as wealthy as the average Chinese, not 11 times as rich, as the conventional numbers suggest.

The different approaches to valuing economic output and resources are not just of theoretical interest. They have real-world significance, especially in the balance of power and economic dominance. The conventional numbers would suggest that the United States has three times the capability of China to mobilize real military resources in the event of a conflict. The numbers based on purchasing-power parity suggest that conventional estimates considerably exaggerate U.S. capability. To the extent that the service of soldiers and other domestically produced goods and services constitute real military resources, the purchasing-power parity numbers must also be taken into account.

China and Economic Dominance

The economic advantage China is gaining will only widen in the future because China's gross domestic product growth rate will be substantially and consistently greater than that of the United States for the near future. By 2030, I expect the Chinese economy to be twice as large as that of the United States (in purchasing-power parity dollars).

Moreover, China's lead will not be confined to GDP. China is already the world's largest exporter of goods. By 2030, China's trade volume will be twice that of the United States. And, of course, China is also a net creditor to the United States.

The combination of economic size, trade and creditor status will confer on China a kind of economic dominance that the United States enjoyed for about five to six decades after World War II and that Britain enjoyed at the peak of empire in the late 19th century.

This will matter in two important ways. America's ability to influence China will be seriously diminished, which is already evident in China's unwillingness to change its exchange rate policy despite U.S. urging. And the open trading and financial system that the United States fashioned after World War II will be increasingly China's to sustain or undermine.

The new numbers, the underlying realities they represent and the future they portend must serve as a wake-up call for America to get its fiscal house in order and quickly find new sources of economic dynamism if it is not to cede its preeminence to a rising, perhaps already risen, China.

10

In the Future, the US Will Share Economic Power with Many Countries

Ian Bremmer

Ian Bremmer is president of Eurasia Group and author of The End of the Free Market.

While China is certainly a threat to US economic dominance, the real problem is centered on a changing world: In the future, America will have to negotiate with many other economic powers. As Asia emerges and as Europe recovers its economic stability, the United States will no longer be able to assume global dominance. While the recent recession has highlighted this historic shift, the transition has been in the making for several decades. The US economy can continue to prosper, but its success will depend on how well politicians are able to react to the changing landscape of the global market.

Halfway through 2011, we've already seen an extraordinary year of volatility: turmoil across the Middle East and North Africa, the eurozone's ongoing fiscal crises, Japan's triple disaster, the killing of Osama bin Laden. Yet these dramatic events have obscured a slow-moving, underlying shift of much greater long-term importance: global rebalancing. In its simplest form, rebalancing means this: a reset of the global economy shifting the balance of accounts between the world's established and emerging powers or between its biggest consumers and biggest savers. That alone, of course, is a transition of landmark historic significance. Yet it is far from the only consequence, for rebalancing is not just an economic story, but one that will result in a seismic shift in the international balance of power, in every region of the world.

And I have bad news for the United States: Rebalancing won't be the relatively pain-free process some in Washington hope. Faced with an increasingly ugly bilateral trade deficit, many of the most senior U.S. officials—including many who should know better—have repeatedly called on the Chinese leadership to empower Chinese consumers to buy more Chinese-made products and to allow the renminbi, China's currency, to appreciate to help them afford it. The Foreign Policy Survey results reported here also suggest Washington is on solid ground: Nearly 100 percent of the leading economists consulted told the magazine they think the renminbi is undervalued.

In years to come, U.S. diplomats will have to do more than jet around the world twisting arms and cutting deals.

But in reality it's hard to imagine a better example of "be careful what you wish for."

At a moment when Western-led globalization is under threat from a new brand of emerging-market mercantilism, this sort of decoupling will produce a lot of pain. This is what's happening already in many areas of the fast-transforming global economy—but unfortunately, U.S. leaders aren't doing much to prepare for this transition, perhaps because they're in denial about its inevitability and its implications for American power. Talk of "winning the future," whether from President Barack Obama or his Republican rivals, allows Americans to believe that all their country needs is to become more "competitive." But rebalancing means that the U.S. economy can't simply grow its way back to the pre-financial crisis era of American profligacy. Instead, it will have to thrive in a new world in which U.S. primacy is no longer a given.

A New Role for the U.S.

In years to come, U.S. diplomats will have to do more than jet around the world twisting arms and cutting deals. They'll have to find creative solutions to transnational problems that involve multiple players who don't necessarily accept U.S. leadership. American power has always been a mix of hard and soft forms of persuasion: a blend of liberal values, military muscle, and economic leverage. Those values endure, even if the United States itself might not always be loved in foreign capitals. It's the third element of power that is fast waning: the paramount position of the United States in a global economic order built to its advantage. For decades, American consumers have been the engine of growth around the world, and the U.S. economy remains by far the world's largest, two and a half times the size of China's. But the latest projections from the International Monetary Fund forecast that China will surpass the United States by 2016. And China is far from the only rising power on the horizon.

American consumer purchasing power will continue to be an important variable for global growth and the economic health of many countries, but Americans won't have as much money to spend. The financial crisis pulled huge amounts of money from the pockets of U.S. consumers by, among other things, deflating the value of their biggest asset: their homes. And the loss in U.S. purchasing power will be felt in every economy that depends on access to U.S. markets. That's exactly why Chinese policymakers are now working to de-couple—not because Washington wants them to, but because excessive long-term dependence on U.S. consumers puts China's future growth trajectory at risk.

The dollar's preeminent position may be the first casualty of this shift. The United States borrows about $4 billion per day, much of it from China. That borrowing finances the ballooning U.S. debt—in effect, China loans Americans the money that allows them to live beyond their means (and, of course, purchase Chinese goods). But the meltdown in U.S. financial markets and the dive into recession persuaded many within China's leadership that this system is unsustainable. China's domestic economy can no longer depend quite so heavily on foreign consumers to drive the creation of domestic jobs. As China works to stoke the growth of domestic consumption by investing more of its cash at home, the renminbi will appreciate against the dollar and Americans will pay higher prices until cheaper alternatives become available. And as China develops a consumption-driven economy, Chinese consumers will increasingly be spending their hard-earned cash abroad, leading to the development of deeper and more liquid renminbi debt markets, a necessary prerequisite for China's currency to become a leading global reserve currency. This will be a gradual process, but it will come at the expense of the dollar and the big-spending habits its preeminence enables for both U.S. consumers and their government.

The American way of capitalism itself is now under threat.

Washington's security role in East Asia has long paid economic dividends as the United States has translated its military ties into greater trade and investment throughout the region. But as China's consumer markets take on added weight and Americans see their purchasing power reduced by the need to restore the country to long-term fiscal health, East Asian countries will trade increasingly with one another and with fast-growing China. It's already happening. According to Xinhua, China's state-run news agency, "China became the largest trading partner and the single biggest export market of Southeast Asian countries in 2010." China's free trade agreement with the 10 countries of the Association of Southeast Asian Nations, which came into effect last year, is the world's largest in terms of population, and it underscores Washington's inability to continue in its traditional role of free trade champion.

The Reduction of American Influence

Then there is the reform process in Europe, which also threatens to undermine the dollar in the long run. Of course, America's traditional ties with Europe and the enormous trade volumes moving in both directions across the Atlantic demand U.S. support for a strong European economy. But if Europe's resilient core economies can help build a coordinated European fiscal policy and buttress cash-strapped governments like those of Greece, Ireland, Portugal, and other so-called peripheral countries, a strengthened euro can offer another viable alternative to the dollar as a reserve currency. And a recovered eurozone will further weaken America's ability to act as global lender of last resort, reduce the central role of the United States in the global banking system, and further erode America's singular international influence.

Indeed, the American way of capitalism itself is now under threat. That model was built on open market access and minimal government meddling. But the world loves a winner: China's heavily top-down approach is finding adherents from Vietnam to Venezuela, while the idea of American-style market-driven capitalism has lost some of its allure. As the appeal of state-driven capitalism grows, we can expect a much less efficient global economy. We'll see politics injected into economic policymaking much more often and on a much larger scale—within both emerging and established powers.

We'll see governments defend their political interests with new sets of tools and weapons, like currency policies, market access, intellectual property rights, and new forms of resource nationalism that move beyond oil, gas, metals, and minerals into commodities like food.

For Americans, what this all means is that the long, postwar party is over. The U.S. debt-to-GDP ratio has climbed above 84 percent, putting America's ability to meet its obligations in question for the first time in memory. To close the gap, U.S. consumers will have to pay higher taxes, save more money, delay retirement, and accept less generous pension and health-care benefits.

In coming years, an increasingly cash-strapped U.S. government will have to become more sensitive to the costs and risks of its foreign adventures. It will be harder to persuade more cost-conscious Americans (and their lawmakers) that the stability of countries such as Afghanistan, Iraq, or even a longtime U.S. protectorate like Taiwan is worth a bloody and costly fight. Questions will arise abroad about the U.S. commitment to the security of particular regions, encouraging local players to test American resolve and exploit any weakness they find.

Rebalancing will upend lots of assumptions, in the United States and around the world, about American economic resilience and its importance for other countries.

Adapting to a New World

Then there are the economic risks. The dollar has provided the global economy with a deep, liquid, and stable reserve currency that reduces costs and increases efficiency for enormous volumes of commercial transactions. It has offered investors a safe port during many a financial storm, including the 2008 financial crisis. But other governments have already begun to move toward a more diversified basket of currencies and commodities to hold in reserve, weakening confidence in the dollar's long-term dominance. Europe will eventually recover, boosting the euro, and a big wave—a sharp spike in crude-oil prices or another deep and lasting U.S. recession, for example—will only accelerate the global drive to diversify. Borrowing costs in the United States will rise, in part because there will be fewer lenders. The cost of doing business will increase along with the complexity of settling transactions in a world of multiple currencies.

Some might argue that the impact of the relative decline of the U.S. economy has already been felt and that a weaker dollar will ultimately make American products more competitive abroad. *FP's* survey results seem to reflect this optimistic view, though the vast majority of those surveyed are clamoring for rebalancing, with all its pitfalls and dangers. There is no reason to doubt, moreover, the long-term resilience of America's political and economic systems. Democracy offers a degree of domestic political legitimacy that cannot be earned in any other way. America's achievements in higher education and innovation are, and will remain, the envy of much of the rest of the world.

But rebalancing will upend lots of assumptions, in the United States and around the world, about American economic resilience and its importance for other countries. This transition is not a product of poor decisions or myopic political leadership—though leaders of both parties in Washington have offered plenty of both in recent years. This is a structural shift, one that has been decades in the making. Resistance is futile. Adapting to its impact can help Americans, and everyone else, thrive in the era to come.

11

A Long-Term View of the US Economy

Matthew Bandyk

Matthew Bandyk is a reporter for U.S. News & World Report.

When making predictions, many observers focus on the near future. Author Joel Kotkin, however, has based his predictions on the year 2050. At that time, he believes, gas shortages will become more common, creating greener and more varied urban landscapes. With new technology, many people will also be able to work from home, a choice that will allow Americans to live wherever they wish to live. On the world scene, China's economic threat will lesson as its population ages. With all of these fluctuations, many aspects of American life will appear transformed by the year 2050.

Think back to 1967. The job you have today may not even have existed. The Internet, and all the jobs that have come with it, were decades away. The Detroit automakers were dominant. Quality of life was different, too: The median household income was an inflation-adjusted $40,261, compared with $50,303 in 2008. There were also a hundred million fewer of us; 1967 was the year the U.S. population hit 200 million. We passed the 300 million mark in 2006, and by 2050, there will very likely be more than 400 million Americans. The lifestyle of the average American may change just as much from 2010 to 2050 as it did from 1967 to 2006. The economy will especially undergo change. . . .

Joel Kotkin, distinguished presidential fellow in urban futures at Chapman University, has spent a lot of time thinking about exactly what those changes might look like in 2050. He previously wrote a book about the history of American cities, but in his new book, *The Next Hundred Million: America in 2050*, he looks ahead to how recent economic and demographic trends may play out over the next few decades. Here are a few of the book's most striking predictions.

1. *The death of the suburbs is highly exaggerated.* In the 20th century, the suburbs became the primary place for Americans to live. But the recent housing market crash, high gas prices, and concerns about environmental sustainability have caused many to wonder how long suburbs will be able to grow. Kotkin writes that the suburbs will not only continue to grow; they will become even more like cities. "The suburbs of the future will in many ways be more diverse than the cities," Kotkin told *U.S. News*. While the suburbs of the 1950s were predominantly white, suburbs today have an increasing number of ethnic minorities and recent immigrants. A major reason suburbs are changing is that they are providing more jobs than ever. Historically, people living in bedroom communities outside of a city have commuted downtown to work. Suburbs are also becoming more appealing because they are developing their own cultural amenities. "Many have rebuilt town centers and revived Main Streets," says Kotkin.

This growth will be made possible—and desirable, Kotkin argues—because suburbs will become what he calls "greenurbia." Kotkin predicts that while cars will continue to be the dominant mode of transportation, fuel-economy improvements, more energy-efficient homes, and telecommuting will allow suburbs to coexist with a clean environment.

2. *The rise of "luxury cities."* Cities, however, are not on the way out. Kotkin points to New York and San Francisco as models for some cities in the future: expensive places that are playgrounds for younger and often single residents. This is one trend that Kotkin finds worrisome. "New York has got to be able to hold on to enough middle-class people, ages 30 to 45," he says. The "luxury city" also creates problems for residents' upward mobility. Kotkin's chief concern is that even as more ethnic minorities join the middle class, the ability for people in the middle class to enjoy the same lifestyle as the upper class in their cloistered cities will be limited. "Class, not race, is going to be the great American issue," says Kotkin.

In the next 50 years, Americans will more often choose their communities and cities based on where they want to live, not where they want to work.

---

3. *Jobs get more virtual.* Jobs are perhaps the biggest concern of Americans today. Kotkin looks to new businesses that began during the recession to point the way to the future of jobs. "There has been a huge surge in the number of independent proprietorships," says Kotkin. Thanks to the Internet, the average entrepreneur does not need a large corporation in an office building to run a business and can instead find people to help run the business online. "Some of these jobs are going to places like China and India, but they are also going to places like North Dakota," says Kotkin.

That's not to say that physical locations for businesses will be unnecessary or that rural towns in the heartland can be just as innovative as large metropolitan areas. "You'll still have centers. Wall Street will still be a center of finance, for example. Their market shares will reduce over time, however," says Kotkin.

4. *The decline of mobility.* Moving companies might not be the biggest boom industry this century. If you don't work

from an office, you don't need to live in a particular city. Kotkin predicts that in the next 50 years, Americans will more often choose their communities and cities based on where they want to live, not where they want to work. "Once they find where they want to be, they will be less likely to move," he says. That decline in mobility would be a big change from the trend over the past 50 years, when it became common for Americans to move many times in their lifetime. Demographics provide another reason moving might decline: Aging baby boomers are more likely to stay put.

5. *Less to fear from China.* America is becoming a more elderly country, but it's not alone. Demographics, Kotkin argues, will prevent China from eclipsing the United States as an economic superpower, as some have predicted. In the late 1980s and early 1990s, Kotkin disagreed with people who feared that the Japanese economy was going to outcompete America. Today, he says similar claims about the Chinese economy are just as overblown. The United Nations has projected that in 2050, 31 percent of China will be over age 60, compared with 25 percent in the United States. Because of its aging populace, China will have to spend more to care for the elderly and deal with workforce shortages. The United States will surely face those problems with baby boomers, but Kotkin argues that America is better equipped to handle its aging citizens than China. "We have a little more of a head start. Our older people have quite a bit more money," he says. China will still be a superpower, Kotkin says—but it will share that status with the United States and India.

12

US Housing May Prompt an Economic Recovery

The Economist

The Economist *is an international news magazine published in the United Kingdom.*

While the US housing market remains weak, it still has the potential to revive the country's economy, helping to create more jobs and lead to more investment confidence. One clear sign of an improvement is an increased use of rental properties. In itself, an increase in rentals can help spur housing starts. Many problems, however, remain on the horizon, including the euro crisis (a problem with excessive debt and austerity measures in a number of European Union nations). Even with these potential problems, the housing market will eventually recover, spurring new growth in the US economy.

There are two things everyone knows about American economic recoveries. The first is that the housing sector traditionally leads the economy out of recession. The second is that there is no chance of the housing sector leading the present economy anywhere, except deeper into the mire. In the two years after the recession of the early 1980s housing investment rose 56%; it is down 6.3% in the present recovery. America is saddled with a debilitating overhang of excess housing, the thinking goes, and as a result is doomed to years of slow growth and underemployment.

The economic landscape is unquestionably littered with the wreckage of the crash. Home prices languish near post-bubble lows, over 30% below peak. The plunge in prices has left nearly a quarter of all mortgage borrowers owing more than the value of their homes; nearly 10m [million] are seriously delinquent on their loans or in foreclosure. The hardest-hit markets are ghost neighbourhoods, filled with dilapidated properties. Housing markets are far from healthy. Yet current pessimism seems overdone. A turnaround in sales, prices and construction may be closer than many imagine.

Although total housing supply is not far out of line, the distribution of supply between the rental and owner-occupied markets remains distorted.

The Housing Recovery

The potential for a strong housing recovery lies in the depths of the bust. America's housing boom was remarkable for its impact on prices and for the flow of new households into the market, which pushed the home-ownership rate above 69%, the highest on record. Construction also boomed, but less wildly. Housing completions were above average during the boom, but not unusually so, particularly in light of the relatively restrained growth in housing supply during the 1990s. . . . The bust, by contrast, dragged new construction to unprecedented depths. At the current rate, fewer homes will be added to the housing stock this year than in any year since records began in 1968.

America therefore has only a minor problem of excess housing supply. Under normal conditions, that small glut would quickly have disappeared in a bust on the present scale. But America is now adding new households at a rate well below normal—not because the population is growing more slowly, but because, for example, young people are opting to stay longer in their parents' home. According to one analysis, there are now 1.5m more young adults (aged 18 to 34) living at home than would be expected, given long-term trends. Thrift imposed by a sickly economy is probably the principal cause. Better prospects for young adults would encourage the forming of new households, buoying the demand for new homes.

Although total housing supply is not far out of line, the distribution of supply between the rental and owner-occupied markets remains distorted. In September the inventory of newly built houses for sale fell to its lowest level since record-keeping began. But the inventory of existing houses, while falling, remains high. In September the figure dipped below 3.5m, down from over 4.5m in 2008 but still above the 2.5m registered early in the last decade. The total number of vacant homes for sale has steadily declined and is at the lowest level since 2006. But the pace of sales remains extraordinarily low, and foreclosures will continue to prevent a faster decline in inventory.

The Rental Market

Rental markets, by contrast, look far stronger. America's rental vacancy rate stood at 9.8% in the third quarter of 2011, down from a high above 11% in 2009. Vacancy rates in some cities are strikingly low—2.4% in New York City, for instance, and 3.6% in San Francisco—which translates into rising rents. Nationally, rents rose 2.1% in the year to August [2011], in stark contrast to house prices. . . .

Housing markets could lurch sharply downwards if a new shock, perhaps from Europe, disturbed the global economy.

Strength in the market for rentals is beginning to seep into the more troubled owner-occupied sector. Rising rents help housing markets heal on both the supply and demand side, by encouraging renters to consider buying and through the movement of supply into the rental market, easing the glut of houses for sale. The Obama administration hopes to take advantage of better rental conditions to unload some of the more than 200,000 foreclosed-on homes held by the two government-sponsored mortgage giants, Fannie Mae and Freddie Mac, and the Federal Housing Administration (which account for roughly half of all such inventory), on to investors who may rent the properties out.

Rental-market strength is also rousing a long-dormant building industry. New housing starts rose 15% from August to September of this year, driven by a 53% surge in new structures containing five units or more. In the three months to September construction employment rose by 29,000 jobs. The sector is still some 2.2m jobs below its pre-recession peak, and new hiring there would help a dismal labour market.

A Stranglehold on Lending

The convalescence, however, may be complicated. Housing recoveries have seemed imminent before, only to peter out when the economic outlook weakened. Foreclosures are falling, but they continue to place downward pressure on prices. New proposals from the administration aim to help underwater borrowers refinance, but more lavish assistance for troubled borrowers is too politically unpopular and expensive for Washington's taste.

The macroeconomic environment, too, remains troublesome. Housing markets could lurch sharply downwards if a new shock, perhaps from Europe, disturbed the global economy. A new financial shock could rattle confidence and send buyers fleeing, while the flow of mortgage credit from exposed banks would dry up. Lenders carry the scars of the housing crash. Cautious banks are reluctant to lend. Housing-finance institutions, having kept credit standards too loose during the bubble, now seem to be setting them too tight, preventing rising demand and low rates from translating into new sales.

Yet once the housing sector finds its footing it may quickly gain momentum. A switch from falling to rising prices should encourage banks to make more loans. Higher house values would chip away at negative equity, stanching the flow of defaults and foreclosures.

A new analysis by Goldman Sachs argues that housing can "punch above its weight" in recoveries. Rising house values boost confidence and spending, and home construction is more labour-intensive than other sectors. A housing recovery should also give monetary policy more traction; low interest rates do less to perk up the economy when housing markets are depressed. Indeed, the Federal Reserve is considering nudging recovery along by buying mortgage assets, which should ease the flow of credit to borrowers.

Such hopes for housing would smack of an effort to reanimate a corpse, had the bust not so far outpaced the boom. But a turnaround now seems probable on many measures. If it happens, the recovery should become much more vigorous.

13

The US Recession Continues to Impact Children

Julia B. Isaacs

Julia B. Isaacs is a fellow at the Brookings Institution focusing on child and family policy issues.

Because of the US recession, more American children have fallen into poverty. Often this occurs when one or more parent loses a job. Unfortunately, even as the current recession came to an end, the effects of poverty have continued to impact children. Poverty rates can be measured by looking at the number of people receiving government nutrition assistance. While these statistics vary from state to state, the overall number of children receiving assistance has nearly doubled since the recession began in 2007. Even with an improved economic scenario in the near future, the demand for nutritional assistance will remain high.

The country is slowly emerging from the Great Recession, the longest period of economic downturn since the Great Depression of the 1930s. During the first nine moths of 2011, the national unemployment averaged 9.0 percent, a distressingly high rate, even though this is down from the 9.6 percent average in 2010 and the peak of 10.1 percent in October 2009.

While the recession is technically over, our nation's children continue to be negatively impacted by its lingering effects. Children in every state are experiencing the effects of the recession, with children in some states hit harder than others.

The impact of the recession on children can be hard to see. Unemployment statistics released by the Bureau of Labor Statistics rarely mention the millions of children living in families with unemployed parents. And while poverty statistics include child poverty rates, there is a significant time lag in their release. For example, child poverty rates for 2011 will not be released until September 2012.

Parental job loss can harm children in a number of different ways.

Many policy makers and child advocates would prefer more current measures of child poverty and economic hardship, in order to assess the needs of children and their families in the current time period. This brief responds by providing updated statistics on three indicators of child economic well-being; children with an unemployed parent, individuals receiving nutrition assistance benefits, and child poverty. These indicators are tracked for all 50 states and the District of Columbia (hereafter referred to as a state), using the most up-to-date information, including the author's predictions for child poverty in 2011.

Children with an Unemployed Parent

Unemployment averaged 9.0 percent in the first nine months of 2011, leaving an average monthly count of 12.7 million Americans out of work. Three out of ten (30 percent) of these unemployed individuals are parents, resulting in millions of children with unemployed parents.

Parental job loss can harm children in a number of different ways. Most obviously, sharp declines in family income can lead to economic hardship and poverty, particularly if the family's income was low prior to the job loss or if unemployment lasts for a long period. In addition, unemployed parents often experience psychological distress, which tends to diminish their parenting capacity, and can lead to child abuse in some cases. Negative effects on children can persist long after the period of unemployment ends, with effects seen on grade repetition and educational attainment, the child's aspirations for his or her own future success in the labor market, and the child's earnings upon reaching adulthood.

An estimated 6.5 million children under the age of 18 are living in families with an unemployed parent during an average month of 2011, based on data through the first nine months of the year. This is a significant increase from the 3.8 million children with unemployed parents in December 2007, the month in which the nation technically entered into recession. On a more positive note, the number of children with unemployed parents has dropped between 2010 and 2011 and is considerably lower than in December 2009, when the unemployment rate was 10.0 percent and 8.1 million children lived with a parent looking for work.

By 2011, one in seven Americans—14 percent—were receiving [nutritional assistance] benefits, a dramatic increase from 9 percent in 2007.

There are over 1 million children of unemployed parents in California, which has the second highest state unemployment rate in 2011 (12 percent, second only to Nevada at 13 percent, based on data through the first nine months of the year). The percentage of children living with an unemployed parent ranges from 3 percent in North Dakota to 13 percent in Nevada, averaging 9 percent nationwide. . . .

One of the more troubling aspects of the current economy is the number of long-term unemployed, that is, individuals who are unemployed for six months or longer. More than 3 million children are living with a long-term unemployed parent during an average month of 2011. This represents almost half (47 percent) of all children living with unemployed parents. Children in California, Florida, Michigan and Nevada are more likely than children in other states to be living with parents who have been out of work for six months or longer.

Nutrition Assistance

As the economy has worsened in the past few years, more Americans have signed up to receive food stamps, or what are now called Supplemental Nutrition Assistance Program (SNAP) benefits. The old paper food stamps have been replaced by plastic electronic benefit cards, which function like ATM cards, and allow families to purchase food at grocery stores. Between June 2007 and June 2011, the number of people receiving nutrition assistance benefits grew by 70 percent, or 18.4 million people, as monthly caseloads averaged over the first six months of the year skyrocketed from 26.2 million to 44.5 million participants. By 2011, one in seven Americans—14 percent—were receiving SNAP benefits, a dramatic increase from 9 percent in 2007.

The percentage of Americans receiving SNAP benefits rose rapidly in the second half of 2008, a few months after the unemployment rates started rising. While unemployment rates peaked in late 2009, the SNAP recipiency rate has continued rising through 2010 and 2011, although the recent increases are not as steep as in 2009. . . .

SNAP caseloads are used as an indicator of economic well-being among children because almost half (47 percent) of all SNAP participants are children and another quarter (27 percent) are adults living in households with children. Roughly 8 million more children were receiving SNAP benefits in the spring of 2011 than four years earlier, bringing the total number of child recipients to 21 million children or more than one in four American children.

The Growth of Government Aid

In one sense, the rise in SNAP benefits can be viewed positively, as a sign that the safety net is working: families suffering economic decline as a result of the recession are receiving assistance so that their children do not go hungry. On the other hand, the rise in SNAP caseloads signals the rising needs of families, particularly families with children. Helping parents to meet the needs of the children in these families may require more than a monthly nutrition assistance benefit averaging $134 per person.

Child poverty has risen by a percentage point or more for each of the last four years, rising from 18 percent in 2007 to 22 percent in 2010.

All 51 states have seen dramatic growth in SNAP caseloads between 2007 and 2011. Caseloads more than doubled in eight states: Delaware, Florida, Idaho, Maryland, Nevada, Rhode Island, Utah and Wisconsin. . . . While much of this growth occurred in the early years of the recession, SNAP caseloads continued to grow between 2010 and 2011 across the nation. . . .

To allow comparisons across states of different sizes, it is useful to track changes in recipiency rates, defined as average monthly participation divided by state population. Recipiency rates range from 7 percent in Wyoming to 22 percent in the District of Columbia in 2011. . . . The nation's capital is not the only jurisdiction where one in five people are receiving SNAP benefits; one-fifth of the state population is also receiving SNAP benefits in Michigan, Mississippi, New Mexico, Oregon and Tennessee.

While increased economic need is the primary driving factor behind increases in SNAP caseloads, shifts in policy and administrative practices also can affect caseloads. Indeed there have been a number of changes in recent years that might lead to increased SNAP caseloads, including greater use of online applications, the adoption by many states of broad-based categorical eligibility, and an expansion in maximum benefits in April 2009. . . . The combination of eligiblity expansions and increased take-up rates among eligible families increased participant caseloads by about 7 percent between 2007 and 2009. While substantial, this growth represents less than a third of the total (26 percent) growth in caseloads over those same two years. Most of the dramatic caseload growth from 2007 to 2011, therefore, represents deteriorating economic conditions and increased economic hardship among children. However, administrative practices may explain trends in particular states.

There is disturbing evidence that poverty has negative effects on children's development, with some effects persisting into adulthood.

Child Poverty Rates

Child poverty is perhaps the most direct measure of children's economic well-being. Child poverty has risen by a percentage point or more for each of the last four years, rising from 18 percent in 2007 to 22 percent in 2010. Over the same three years, the number of poor children has increased by 3 million, from 13 million to 16 million. These poverty statistics are based on traditional Census Bureau poverty measures, which count the number and percentage of children living in families with annual cash incomes below the official poverty threshold, which was about $17,000 for a family of three and $22,000 for a family of four in 2010.

The rise in child poverty during the current recession is consistent with the pattern of the past 50 years, in which poverty rates for children and working-age adults have tended to rise and fall with changes in unemployment rates. . . . In contrast, elderly poverty has declined over the past 50 years, as Social Security and Supplemental Security Income have done much to reduce the problem of elderly poverty.

Peak levels of child poverty frequently occur a year or so after peak levels of unemployment, giving a preliminary indication that child poverty is likely to rise again in 2011. The state-by-state predictions in this paper suggest that national child poverty will rise by an estimated 0.5 percentage points in 2011, a small but statistically significant increase that will leave the rounded rate at 22 percent. These predictions may be conservative; other Brookings researchers have run simulations suggesting the child poverty may be as high as 24 percent in 2011.

Most states (43 states) had markedly higher poverty rates in 2010 than during the pre-recessionary period.

The high rate of child poverty—more than one in five children—is troubling. In addition to humanitarian concerns about the immediate well-being of children, there is disturbing evidence that poverty has negative effects on children's development, with some effects persisting into adulthood. There are several pathways through which poverty may influence child development. With less family income, children in poor families may lack the resources needed for healthy development, such as having access to nutritious meals and enriched home environments. Poor children also may suffer from the negative effects of living in neighborhoods with more crime and air and noise pollution. Poverty also can affect the psychological well-being of parents, contributing to depression and other forms of psychological stress that can negatively impact their interactions with children. Even when parental stress does not manifest itself in observed changes in mental health, it can contribute to a harsh and less supportive parenting style. While social scientists are still exploring which pathway is most important in explaining why poverty is so bad for children, there is general consensus that the lingering negative effects of poverty are strongest when poverty is experienced during early childhood, when poverty lasts for several years of childhood, or both.

Child Poverty Variations

Child poverty rates vary dramatically across the states, ranging from 32.5 percent in Mississippi to 10.0 percent in New Hampshire in 2010. . . . That is, nearly three in ten children in Mississippi, compared to about one in ten children in New Hampshire, lived in families with annual cash incomes below the national poverty thresholds. Three states had child poverty rates of 30 percent or higher: the District of Columbia, Mississippi and New Mexico.

Before the recession, states with high child poverty rates were generally clustered in the southern and southwestern regions of the country. . . . The 14 states with poverty rates of 20 percent or higher in the pre-recessionary period included Alabama, Arizona, Arkansas, the District of Columbia, Kentucky, Louisiana, Mississippi, New Mexico, North Carolina, Oklahoma, South Carolina, Tennessee, Texas, and West Virginia. (Poverty before the recession is measured as the average child poverty rate over 2000–2007). By 2009, the number of "high poverty" states had swollen to 22 states, including the original 14 states plus a geographically diverse set of eight additional states that had child poverty rates of at least 20 percent: Georgia, Florida, Indiana, Michigan, Missouri, Montana, New York, and Ohio. By 2010, three western states had joined the ranks of high poverty states—California, Nevada and Oregon—bringing the total to 25 states.

The highest increases were in Michigan, Indiana, and Nevada, where child poverty was more than 6 percentage points higher in 2010 than average levels before the recession. Most states (43 states) had markedly higher poverty rates in 2010 than during the pre-recessionary period. . . . A few states experienced increases (5 states) or decreases (3 states) that were within the margin of error around the estimates for 2010.

Note that even though the American Community Survey has a large sample of households in every state and is the best available source of data on child poverty at the state level, child poverty estimates have a margin of error that is between 0.4 and 1.5 percentage points for two-thirds of the states (37 states), and even larger for less populated states (between 1.6 and 2.6 percentage points for 12 of the smaller states, and 3.8 percentage points for the District of Columbia). This lack of precision means that smaller states can see changes in reported poverty rates of as much as 2 percentage points without being counted as a state with a real change in the underlying poverty rate.

The economy may have begun its slow recovery, but conditions are not yet improving for children in the most vulnerable families.

The Continued Impact of Child Poverty

Child poverty rates are predicted to rise again in 2011, but by smaller amounts than the past few years, according to a model that predicts child poverty on the basis of unemployment rates, SNAP recipiency rates and lagged child poverty. Under this model . . . , 12 states are predicted to have a rise in child poverty in excess of the margin of error around the 2010 estimates. These dozen states include five states in the South (Florida, Louisiana, Maryland, Texas and Virginia), four states in the Northeast (Connecticut, Massachusetts, New York, and Rhode Island) and three states in the West (California, Idaho and Washington). No state in the Midwest is predicted to have a statistically significant rise in child poverty; in fact, child poverty is projected to decline by at least a percentage point in two midwestern states (Indiana and Nebraska). . . . For two-thirds of the states (37) the change in child poverty be-tween 2010 and 2011 is not large enough to exceed the mar-gin of error surrounding the estimates. . . .

All the states marked as "high child poverty" states . . . are expected to retain that dubious distinction in 2011. Two addi-tional states—Idaho and Rhode Island—are projected to join their ranks, resulting in a projected total of 27 states with child poverty rates of 20 percent or higher in 2011. If these projections are correct, that means a near doubling of the number of states experiencing high child poverty during the recession, from 14 mostly southern and southwestern states to 27 states found throughout the South, much of the West, and portions of the Northeast and Midwest.

The Need for More Assistance

Many families have at least one parent out of work, are turn-ing to SNAP benefits to put food on the table, and/or have cash income less than the poverty threshold ($17,000 per year for a family of three). Two of these three indicators are worse in 2011 than in 2010, indicating a continued deterioration in children's economic well-being. The one positive trend is that the number of children with an unemployed parent in 2011 is lower than a year ago. However, SNAP caseloads continue to rise, and child poverty also is rising, according to the predic-tions presented here. The economy may have begun its slow recovery, but conditions are not yet improving for children in the most vulnerable families.

The continued worsening of children's economic well-being comes at a time when both federal and state budgets are tight. A temporary boost in federal spending on children is ending, as the one-time funds enacted under the stimulus package of February 2009 are gradually exhausted. State bud-gets are still struggling to recover from the recession, making it difficult for state governments to maintain, let alone expand, their assistance to children and families. At the same time, there are loud calls in Congress for large cuts in federal spending.

The indicators of child well-being presented in this brief provide important contextual background for the ongoing debates over federal and state budgets. As policy makers engage in debates over the size of government spending, the appropriate mix of spending cuts and tax increases to address the budget deficits, and the timing of any proposed budget cuts, it is important to acknowledge that many families with children have not yet recovered from the recession and are in greater need of government assistance than in normal economic times.

14

Economic Realities May Make Retirement More Difficult

Matt Krantz

Matt Krantz is a market reporter for USA Today *newspaper.*

Today, many Americans have managed to save very little toward retirement. As a result, many will continue working, putting off retirement until later ages. Even many of those who have saved lost large sums during the stock market crash of 2008. While Americans need to plan for retirement, the current US economic problems have made planning more difficult. Increasingly, there is also the prospect that many Americans will never be able to retire.

For many Americans, the golden years are quickly taking on a tin-like hue.

After a vicious decade of no growth for the stock market, including two 401(k)-eating bear markets and persistently sky-high unemployment, more Americans are finding themselves in their 50s and 60s with practically no money saved for retirement.

"We were in our 30s, blinked, and now we're our parents' age," says Alan Tipps, a corporate jet pilot who typically earns more than $100,000 a year when he's working. But Tipps, 52, has been laid off three times during the past four years, and says that has forced him to burn through what was in his 401(k) just to "keep the lights on" in his home in Portales, N.M.

Investors of all ages have suffered. But for those close to retirement, it's been especially tough, because they're faced with taking distributions from investment portfolios that in some cases are a fraction of their peak value. Forced early retirements and the near extinction of pensions are making things worse, creating a generation of aging investors in which some have little or no plans for how they're going to pay for retirement.

More than half of retirees, 54%, report they have less than $25,000 saved.

It gets more ominous, given the other changes Americans are facing. Declining property values have drained home equity that many retirees might have counted on. Meanwhile, the number of people reaching retirement age is soaring as the Baby Boom generation ages.

Saving early and often is the way Americans typically fund their retirement, the biggest financial obligation most will face. Pensions for many have become a thing of the past. Retirement needs vary greatly, but the numbers are universally huge. A 65-year-old retiree would need to have $1.1 million saved to draw $50,000 a year in inflation-adjusted dollars, assuming 3% inflation and a 5% annual return from investments. That's if the investor is lucky enough to get a 5% return, which, given the flat-line returns of stocks the last decade, might give some pause.

Meanwhile, data show that many workers nearing retirement age have saved nowhere near the amount they need, and many have very little savings. More than half of all workers, 56%, say they have less than $25,000 in savings, according to a survey by the Employee Benefit Research Institute.

And the strain is already starting to show up as more Americans actually retire. More than half of retirees, 54%, report they have less than $25,000 saved. That's up dramatically from 2006, when 42% said they had less than that.

Financial advisers say they're seeing an increasing number of workers and new retirees with no savings and no plan to dig out of debt.

For many Americans approaching retirement age, the increasing gap in savings is eroding confidence that retirement is even possible. Nearly 30% of workers of all ages surveyed aren't confident they'll have enough to retire, the highest level in the 21 years that EBRI has tracked the statistic. That means 36% of workers now expect to have to keep working after age 65, up from 20% in 2001.

Not only are many Americans close to retirement age lacking savings, some are in the hole financially.

The EBRI survey found that 42% of retirees say their current level of debt is a problem.

Double Whammy

Financial advisers say they're seeing an increasing number of workers and new retirees with no savings and no plan to dig out of debt. "There are a lot more people behind the eight ball," says Joel Redmond, a financial planner for Key Private Bank in Syracuse, N.Y.

Redmond and other advisers cite a range of factors jeopardizing retirement today:

Ravages of the stock market. The people Redmond encounters most who are lacking sufficient retirement savings weren't necessarily delinquent or negligent. Many had money saved but were wiped out by the sour stock market in the past decade and poor investment strategies, Redmond says.

That's what happened, in part, to Robert and Connie Cabana of Tampa, who are both in their 60s. Robert built up a sizable 401(k) working as a financial executive at Verizon. Connie was a business assistant for a local irrigation supply company. Connie was laid off four years ago; Robert was let go three years ago.

Baby Boomers, in contrast with their Depression- and World War II-era parents . . . , have looked at savings as a downer.

But the serious hit to their retirement, which wiped out half their 401(k) savings, resulted from the stock market and an overexposure to risky stocks, they say. Now, 75% of their 401(k) is gone, and they have "very little" left, Robert says.

Procrastination and delays in getting retirement savings in place. Baby Boomers, in contrast with their Depression- and World War II-era parents, who typically were good savers and had company pensions, have looked at savings as a downer, says Chris Olsen, 49, a financial planner with Ameriprise.

Many people now in their 50s and 60s with no savings figured they could lean on Social Security for their retirement, he says. In reality, Olsen says, Social Security payments are far from adequate to fund skyrocketing health care costs. The payments also are losing purchasing power relative to inflation, he says. Social Security, in practice, pays for only about 40% of most retirees' needs, says Paul Jarvis, financial adviser at State Bank & Trust in Fargo, N.D.

"I always made a lot of money. I always spent a lot of money. I've done whatever I wanted to do," says Paul Conlin, 53, a contractor in Liverpool, N.Y., who says he has less than $50,000 saved for retirement. "I live for the moment. When I want to do something, I do it."

But after consulting with a financial planner, Conlin, who is married and has three children, is starting to put money away for retirement. He's saving $6,000 a year in a Roth IRA, "and it's growing," he says. "I've changed my habits."

Even so, he's not ready to go crazy on a savings binge, figuring he'll probably keep working well into his 70s or beyond. "If you stop working totally, then you will die."

Coming up with a financial plan, at least, allows people to set realistic expectations for what they need to do.

Putting retirement last. Financial obligations faced by young families can be so crushing that saving for retirement often is the last thing that gets attention, Jarvis says. After paying down debt and paying for kids' college, many Americans find themselves in their 50s with next to no retirement savings, he says.

Unemployment hitting retirement savings plans. Tipps says that while his income is good while he's working, routine layoffs constantly knock his retirement savings plans off course.

"It's good money while you're working," he says. "But it's feast or famine." Unfortunately, since corporate jets are seen as an executive perk, companies are quick to cut them when times get tough. "My retirement plan is the New Mexico state lottery," he jokes.

Make a Plan

Joking aside, it's critical for people in their 50s and 60s to recognize immediately the severity of the situation, Redmond says. Coming up with a financial plan, at least, allows people to set realistic expectations for what they need to do. There are only so many things people in this situation can do, says Redmond. The only variables most people can control are working longer, saving more or getting a higher return on their investments, he says.

Some, such as Conlin, may simply choose to postpone retirement and keep working. He says members of his family routinely live into their 90s, and he's ready to keep working.

In an effort to save more, the Cabanas are attempting to launch a business in which they distribute coffee and chocolate to organizations conducting fundraisers. They're hopeful the business could take off, though sales recently have been soft due to the economy, they say.

The most likely option for many is doing an extreme makeover of their finances and slashing costs.

But working longer might not be an option for some, such as Tipps. He says that insurance carriers that provide coverage for pilots might make the premiums for those older than 65 prohibitively expensive in the future.

Instead, Tipps, is trying to teach himself to be a successful active investor and get a higher rate of return on savings. He's using a practice trading account at an online brokerage to try different active trading strategies using virtual money. If he's successful, he'd like to start for real once he's working steadily again. Tipps is also determined to set up a Roth IRA, a retirement account that lets investors' money grow tax-free.

Perhaps the most likely option for many is doing an extreme makeover of their finances and slashing costs. Olsen and Jarvis have both seen retirees with little money sell their homes in costly parts of the nation and move to less expensive places. Others forgo many of the things Americans dream of doing during retirement, such as travel.

There's no guarantee that even such extreme measures in retirement will help Americans recover from a lifetime of not saving. Making such sacrifices now creates worries many Americans would rather avoid at this stage in their lives.

Connie Cabana cautions young people to learn from her predicament. "Young people need to start saving as soon as they start working," she says. "There are roadblocks you don't see when you're young. You think money will always be there," she says. "But with life, you need to make provisions."

15

Immigration Reform Can Benefit the US Economy

Raul Hinojosa-Ojeda

Raul Hinojosa-Ojeda is an associate professor in the Department of Chicana and Chicano Studies at the University of California, Los Angeles.

Despite increased enforcement, the current US immigration policy has been a failure: illegal immigration has continued unabated. Unfortunately, illegal immigrants are forced to take the lowest paying jobs in an effort to avoid being deported. The low wages paid illegal immigrants, however, drives down all wages. With reform, legalized immigrants would no longer be underpaid, creating an income "floor" that would benefit all American workers. Better paid workers would also be better consumers and tax payers, benefiting the economy in hard-times.

The current enforcement-only approach to unauthorized immigration is not cost effective and has not deterred unauthorized immigrants from coming to the United States when jobs are available. Rather, enforcement-only policies have wasted billions of taxpayer dollars while pushing unauthorized migration further underground. And these policies have produced a host of unintended consequences: more deaths among border crossers, greater demand for people smugglers, less

Raul Hinojosa-Ojeda, "Raising the Floor for American Workers." Center for American Progress, January 7, 2010. Copyright © 2010 by the Center for American Progress. All rights reserved. Reproduced by permission.

"circular migration" in favor of more "permanent settlement" among unauthorized immigrants, and further depressed wages in low-wage labor markets.

Significant declines in unauthorized immigration have historically occurred only during downturns in the U.S. economy when U.S. labor demand is dampened. And declining birth rates in Mexico will likely accomplish what tens of billions of dollars in border enforcement clearly have not: a reduction in the *supply* of migrants from Mexico who are available for jobs in the United States.

High Costs and No Benefits

The number of unauthorized immigrants in the United States has increased dramatically since the early 1990s despite equally dramatic increases in the amount of money the federal government spends on immigration enforcement. The U.S. Border Patrol's annual budget has increased by 714 percent since 1992—the year before the current era of concentrated immigration enforcement along the U.S.-Mexico border—from $326.2 million in Fiscal Year 1992 to $2.7 billion in FY 2009. . . . And the cost ratio of Border Patrol expenditures to apprehensions has increased by 1,041 percent, from $272 per apprehension in FY 1992 to $3,102 in FY 2008. . . . At the same time, the number of Border Patrol agents stationed along the southwest border has grown by 390 percent, from 3,555 in FY 1992 to 17,415 in FY 2009. . . .

Enforcement-only border policies have not stopped or even slowed the pace of unauthorized immigration.

The budget for U.S. Customs and Border Protection, the Border Patrol's parent agency within the Department of Homeland Security, has also increased by 92 percent since DHS' creation in 2003 from $6.0 billion in FY 2003 to $11.3 billion in FY 2009. And the budget for Immigration and Customs Enforcement, DHS' interior-enforcement counterpart to CBP, has increased by 82 percent from $3.3 billion in FY 2003 to $5.9 billion in FY 2009. . . . Yet the unauthorized-immigrant population of the United States has roughly tripled in size over the past two decades, from an estimated 3.5 million in 1990 to 11.9 million in 2008. . . . The number of unauthorized immigrants in the country appears to have declined slightly since 2007 in response to the recession, which began at the end of that year.

The fact is that nearly all unauthorized migrants still eventually succeed in entering the United States despite tens of billions of dollars of immigration-enforcement spending since the early 1990s. Wayne Cornelius and his colleagues at the University of California, San Diego, have conducted a long-term study of unauthorized migration and found that the vast majority of unauthorized immigrants—92 percent to 98 percent—keep trying to cross the border until they make it. Cornelius has concluded that "tightened border enforcement since 1993 has not stopped nor even discouraged migrants from entering the United States. Neither the higher probability of being apprehended by border patrol, nor the sharply increased danger of clandestine entry through deserts and mountainous terrain, has discouraged potential migrants from leaving home"—provided that U.S. jobs are available. Cornelius and his team have also found that far fewer Mexicans are coming to the United States due to the contraction of the job market in the United States with the onset of recession in December 2007.

The Unintended Consequences of Border Enforcement

Enforcement-only border policies have not stopped or even slowed the pace of unauthorized immigration, but they have distorted the migration process in ways that produce unintended consequences that are detrimental to the U.S. economy, American workers, and unauthorized immigrants themselves, including:

Making the southwestern border more lethal. The concentrated border-enforcement strategy has contributed to a surge in migrant fatalities since 1995 by channeling unauthorized migrants through extremely hazardous mountain and desert areas, rather than the relatively safe urban corridors used in the past. The U.S. Government Accountability Office has estimated that the number of border-crossing deaths doubled in the decade following the beginning of enhanced border-enforcement operations. A report released in October 2009 by the American Civil Liberties Union of San Diego & Imperial Counties and Mexico's National Commission of Human Rights estimates that 5,607 migrants died while crossing the border between 1994 and 2008. . . .

The high costs and physical risks of unauthorized entry give immigrants a strong incentive to extend their stays in the United States.

Creating new opportunities for people smugglers. Stronger enforcement on the U.S.-Mexico border has been a bonanza for the people-smuggling industry. Heightened border enforcement has closed safer, traditional routes and made smugglers essential to a safe and successful crossing. Wayne Cornelius' research in rural Mexico shows that more than 9 out of 10 unauthorized migrants now hire smugglers to get them across the border. Use of smugglers was the exception rather than the rule only a decade ago. And the fees that smugglers charge have tripled since 1993. The going rate for Mexicans was between $2,000 and $3,000 per head in January 2006, and there is evidence of a further rise since that time. Yet even at these prices it is economically rational for migrants—and, often, their relatives living in the United

States—to dig deeper into their savings and go deeper into debt to finance illegal entry.

Breaking circular migration and promoting permanent settlement in the United States. The high costs and physical risks of unauthorized entry give immigrants a strong incentive to extend their stays in the United States; and the longer they stay, the more probable it is that they will settle permanently.

Depressing low-wage labor markets. The enhanced enforcement regime moves unauthorized workers further underground, lowering their pay, and ironically, creating a greater demand for unauthorized workers. A 2008 report from the Atlanta Federal Reserve analyzes how this vicious cycle is activated and expands as firms find themselves forced to compete for the supply of cheaper, unauthorized labor. When a firm cuts costs by hiring unauthorized workers for lower wages, its competitors become more likely to hire unauthorized workers for lower wage, as well, in order to benefit from the same cost savings.

The recent history of U.S. immigration policy offers important insights into the economic benefits of providing unauthorized immigrants with legal status.

Demographic Trends in Mexico

Migration flows from Mexico to the United States can be explained in large part by differences in labor demand and wages between the two countries, but economists also estimate that about one-third of total immigration from Mexico over the past four decades is the result of higher Mexican birth rates. But Mexico has begun to experience what will soon be a major reduction in the supply of new entrants into the North American labor force.

The birth rate in Mexico has fallen from nearly seven children per mother in the mid-1960s to just 2.2 today, barely above replacement rate and only slightly higher than the U.S. level of 2.1. Mexico's birth rate is expected to fall below replacement level over the coming decade. This is one of the fastest declines in fertility ever recorded in any nation. Mexico's working-age population was growing by 1 million each year in the 1990s, when unauthorized migration from Mexico reached record levels. But today that growth rate is only 500,000.

The United States will continue to attract many Mexicans seeking higher wages and a better life, but the population pressures of the past two decades are already starting to recede, and a reduction in the pressures to immigrate to the United States will likely follow. An early indication of this shift is seen in the increasing age of apprehended migrants. The share of apprehended immigrants under the age of 25 was 3.0 percentage points lower in 2008 compared to 2005, while the share of those over the age of 35 was 2.5 percentage points higher.

The Immigration Reform and Control Act (IRCA)

The recent history of U.S. immigration policy offers important insights into the economic benefits of providing unauthorized immigrants with legal status and the drawbacks of immigration reform efforts that are not sufficiently comprehensive in scope.

The 1986 IRCA granted legal status to 1.7 million unauthorized immigrants through its "general" legalization program, plus another 1.3 million through a "Special Agricultural Workers" program. Even though IRCA was implemented during an economic recession characterized by high unemployment, studies of immigrants who benefited from the general legalization program indicate that they soon earned higher wages and moved on to better jobs—and invested more in their own education so that they could earn even higher wages and get even better jobs.

Higher wages translate into more tax revenue and increased consumer purchasing power, which benefits the public treasury and the U.S. economy as a whole. IRCA failed, however, to create flexible limits on future immigration that were adequate to meet the growing labor needs of the U.S. economy during the 1990s. As a result, unauthorized immigration eventually resumed in the years after IRCA, thereby exerting downward pressure on wages for all workers in low-wage occupations.

Legalized Workers Earn More

Surveys conducted by Westat, Inc. for the U.S. Department of Labor found that the real hourly wages of immigrants who acquired legal status under IRCA's general legalization program had increased an average of 15.1 percent by 1992—four to five years after legalization in 1987 or 1988. Men experienced an average 13.2 percent wage increase and women a 20.5 percent increase during that period. And economists Sherrie Kossoudji and Deborah Cobb-Clark found using the same survey data that 38.8 percent of Mexican men who received legal status under IRCA had moved on to higher-paying occupations by 1992.

Other researchers have also analyzed this survey data and supplemented it with data from additional sources—such as the 1990 Census and the National Longitudinal Survey of Youth—in an effort to determine how much of the wage increase experienced by IRCA beneficiaries was the result of legalization as opposed to the many other variables that influenced wage levels for different workers in different occupations during the same period of time. The findings of these researchers vary according to their economic models, but the results show uniformly positive results for IRCA beneficiaries:

- Economist Francisco Rivera-Batiz estimated that the very fact of having legal status had resulted in a wage increase of 8.4 percent for male IRCA beneficiaries and

13 percent for female IRCA beneficiaries by 1992—independent of any increase in earning power they might have experienced as a result of acquiring more education, improving their mastery of English, or other factors.

- Economists Catalina Amuedo-Dorante, Cynthia Bansak, and Stephen Raphael estimated that real hourly wages had increased 9.3 percent for male IRCA beneficiaries and 2.1 percent for female IRCA beneficiaries by 1992—independent of broader changes in the U.S. economy that might have affected wage levels generally.

- Kossoudji and Cobb-Clark estimated that legalization had raised the wages of male IRCA beneficiaries 6 percent by 1992—independent of broader changes in the U.S. and California economies that might have affected wage levels generally.

Legal Status Yields Increasing Returns

The experience of IRCA also indicates that legalization greatly increases the incentives for formerly unauthorized workers to invest in themselves and their communities—to the benefit of the U.S. economy as a whole. As Kossoudji and Cobb-Clark explain, the wages of unauthorized workers are generally unrelated to their actual skill level. Unauthorized workers tend to be concentrated in the lowest-wage occupations; they try to minimize the risk of deportation even if this means working for lower wages; and they are especially vulnerable to outright exploitation by unscrupulous employers. Once unauthorized workers are legalized, however, these artificial barriers to upward socioeconomic mobility disappear.

IRCA allowed formerly unauthorized workers with more skills to command higher wages, and also provided a powerful incentive for all newly legalized immigrants to improve their English-language skills and acquire more education so they could earn even more. Kossoudji and Cobb-Clark estimate that if the men who received legal status under IRCA had been "legal" throughout their entire working lives in the United States, their wages by 1992 would have been 24 percent higher because they would have been paid in relation to their actual skill level since arriving in the country and would therefore have had an incentive to improve their skills to further increase their earning power.

A new, easily exploited unauthorized population arose in the United States during the economic boom of the 1990s.

A recent North American Integration and Development, or NAID research project on the 20-year impact of IRCA shows a number of important long-term improvements among previously unauthorized immigrants. The study illustrates that removing the uncertainty of unauthorized status allows legalized immigrants to earn higher wages and move into higher-paying occupations, and also encourages them to invest more in their own education, open bank accounts, buy homes, and start businesses. These are long-term economic benefits that continue to accrue well beyond the initial five-year period examined by most other studies of IRCA beneficiaries.

Effective Immigration Reform

Unauthorized immigration to the United States initially declined following the passage of IRCA. But IRCA failed to create flexible legal limits on immigration that were capable of responding to ups and downs in future U.S. labor demand. It attempted to stop unauthorized immigration through "employer sanctions" that imposed fines on employers who "knowingly" hire unauthorized workers. Yet it was unable to put an end to unauthorized immigration given the U.S. economy's continuing demand for immigrant labor in excess of existing legal limits on immigration, as well as the ready availability of fraudulent identity documents and the inherent difficulty of proving that an employer has "knowingly" hired an unauthorized worker.

A new, easily exploited unauthorized population arose in the United States during the economic boom of the 1990s. And the costs of employer sanctions were passed along to all Latino workers in the form of lower wages—regardless of legal status or place of birth. This resulted from increased anti-Latino discrimination against job applicants who "looked" like they might be unauthorized, and from the increased use of labor contractors by employers who wanted to distance themselves from the risk of sanctions by having someone else hire workers for them—for a price which was ultimately paid by the workers.

The federal government has three basic choices when it comes to immigration reform:

1. *Comprehensive Immigration reform*: Create a pathway to legal status for unauthorized immigrants already living in the United States, and establish new, flexible legal limits on permanent and temporary immigration that respond to changes in U.S. labor demand in the future.

2. *A program for temporary workers only*: Develop a new temporary-worker program for currently unauthorized immigrants and future immigrants that does not include a pathway to permanent status for unauthorized immigrants or more flexible legal limits on permanent immigration in the future.

3. *Mass deportation*: Expel all unauthorized immigrants from the United States and effectively seal the U.S.-Mexico border to future immigration. This is not a realistic scenario, but it is useful for comparison purposes.

We analyze the economic impact of each of these three scenarios over the course of 10 years by taking the historical experience of legalization under IRCA as a starting point and using a computable general equilibrium model. . . .

The comprehensive immigration reform scenario yields the greatest benefits for the U.S. economy—roughly a cumulative $1.5 trillion in additional GDP [gross domestic product] over 10 years—while increasing wages for all workers. A program for temporary workers only produces half the economic gains of comprehensive immigration reform—$792 billion cumulatively over 10 years—and lowers wages for all workers. And mass deportation costs the U.S. economy a $2.6 trillion in lost, cumulative GDP over 10 years and causes widespread job losses, although it increases wages only for less-skilled native-born workers. . . .

Comprehensive immigration reform brings substantial economic gains even in the short run.

The Economic Benefits of Immigration Reform

The results of our modeling . . . suggest that comprehensive immigration reform would increase U.S. GDP by at least 0.84 percent. Note that 0.84 percent is the projected increase in GDP level, not an increase in the long-term growth rate. GDP each year would be 0.84 percent higher than it otherwise would have been. The additional GDP would have equaled $120 billion if reforms were fully effective and their effect fully realized in 2009. Using 10-year GDP projections prepared by the Congressional Budget Office, adding 0.84 percent to CBO-projected GDP each year yields a 10-year cumulative total of at least $1.5 trillion in added GDP, which includes roughly $1.2 trillion in additional consumption and $256 billion in additional investment. . . .

Comprehensive immigration reform brings substantial economic gains even in the short run—during the first three years following legalization. The real wages of newly legalized workers increase by roughly $4,405 per year among those in less-skilled jobs during the first three years of implementation, and $6,185 per year for those in higher-skilled jobs. The higher earning power of newly legalized workers translates into an increase in net personal income of $30 to $36 billion, which would generate $4.5 to $5.4 billion in additional net tax revenue. Moreover, an increase in personal income of this scale would generate consumer spending sufficient to support 750,000 to 900,000 jobs.

Moving unauthorized workers out of a vulnerable underground status strengthens all working families' ability to become more productive.

The wages of native-born workers also increase under the comprehensive immigration reform scenario because the "wage floor" rises for all workers—particularly in industries where large numbers of easily exploited, low-wage, unauthorized immigrants currently work. Wages for native-born U.S. workers increase by roughly $162 per year for the less skilled and $74 per year for the higher-skilled. Under the temporary worker program scenario, wages fall for both less-skilled and higher-skilled native-born U.S. workers. And under the mass deportation scenario, wages for less-skilled native-born workers actually rise, but only at the cost of significantly fewer jobs as the economy contracts and investment declines. . . .

The benefits of additional U.S. GDP growth under the comprehensive immigration reform scenario are spread very broadly throughout the U.S. economy, with virtually every sector expanding. Particularly large increases occur in immigrant-heavy industries such as textiles, ferrous metals, transportation equipment, electronic equipment, motor vehicles and parts, non-electric machinery and equipment, capital goods, mineral products, and construction. In comparison, every sector experiences significantly smaller gains under the temporary worker scenario, while every sector contracts under the mass deportation scenario. . . .

The experience of IRCA and the results of our modeling both indicate that legalizing currently unauthorized immigrants and creating flexible legal limits on future immigration in the context of full labor rights would raise wages, increase consumption, create jobs, and generate additional tax revenue—particularly in those sectors of the U.S. economy now characterized by the lowest wages. This is a compelling economic reason to move away from the current "vicious cycle" where enforcement-only policies perpetuate unauthorized migration and exert downward pressure on already-low wages, and toward a "virtuous cycle" of worker-empowerment in which legal status and labor rights exert upward pressure on wages.

Legalization of the nation's unauthorized workers and new legal limits on immigration that rise and fall with U.S. labor demand would help lay the foundation for robust, just, and widespread economic growth. Moving unauthorized workers out of a vulnerable underground status strengthens all working families' ability to become more productive and creates higher levels of job-generating consumption, thereby laying a foundation for long-term community revitalization, middle-class growth, and a stronger, more equitable national economy.

16

The Age of the American Consumer Is Over

G.S. Evans

G.S. Evans is a writer and translator who divides his time between the Czech Republic and the United States.

Americans have engaged in hyper-consumerism for a number of years. Recent economic setbacks, however, have called the consumer lifestyle into question, leading experts to ask whether Americans will be able to sustain the material comforts of large homes and new cars in the future. Because the US government and businesses have worked hard to create a modern consumer culture, many Americans will find non-consumer options lacking. However, with US debt rising and consumers unable to sustain their lifestyles, the age of American consumerism may be exhausted.

In the wake of the world economic crisis much has been made, both by economists and the American government, of the need for the rest of the world to take up the "burden" of consuming that the United States has been carrying until now. As Barack Obama stated shortly before the Group of 20 meeting in Pittsburgh in September, "We can't go back to an era where the Chinese or the Germans or other countries just are selling everything to us, we're taking out a bunch of credit-card debt or home-equity loans, but we're not selling them anything."

But such thoughts are wishful thinking, as there are unique cultural, economic, and physical reasons why the United States alone has been both willing and able to take this burden upon itself. The fact that it has exhausted itself to the point of ruin in this endeavor presents the world with a crisis that goes beyond the immediate economic recession (or depression), as it also highlights a structural crisis of capitalism in that an economy based on consumerism is, ultimately, a lie.

The American Consumer

The importance of the American consumer—as well as his and her limitations—was underscored by the fact that the financial instrument that triggered the near collapse of the world economy in 2008 was the sub-prime home loan, an instrument designed to maximize consumer activity in the United States. These risky loans were named "sub-prime" because they supplied less credit-worthy clients, especially in the middle and lower classes, an opportunity to achieve a key part of the "American Dream," owning a house.

For most Americans, owning a home is not only synonymous with being a member of the middle-class—of being successful—but on a deeper level with being an adult.

These loans were initially very popular because, at first glance, they seemed to offer very low interest rates; in reality, however, they had two interest rates, one that was quite low in the first couple of years and then a substantially higher one over the following 28 years. Over the long haul these poorer Americans didn't have the resources to keep up the payments on such loans—which in their form and structure resembled the kind of loans traditionally given out by loan sharks.

That such loans were allowed into the main-stream of the American financial sector, thereby allowing the lenders to draw in many borrowers who trusted that there were laws or regulations against such deceptive loans, says much about the debasement of consumer rights in the United States. That so many Americans, however, took out such loans at all, and thereby allowed the corrupt and rapacious American financial sector to expropriate their limited savings and meager assets, speaks both to the exuberance as well as the irrationality of the American consumer. It also, as we shall see, speaks to the opportunity that their physical environment gives them to consume on such a scale.

The Home and Consumption

These qualities are perhaps best illustrated by the goal that motivated the Americans who took out the sub-prime mortgages, the goal of owning their own home. For most Americans, owning a home is not only synonymous with being a member of the middle-class—of being successful—but on a deeper level with being an adult. For, while the United States does indeed rank highly relative to other countries in terms of official homeownership (69% of Americans own their own home, far above France's 55%, Germany's 42%, and Switzerland's 36%, but comparable with the UK and below Norway's 77%), when discussing homeownership in the United States, we are really talking about "house" ownership, and consistent with this the average owner-occupied housing unit in the United States in 2001 was almost half again larger than owner-occupied units in Germany and France, and almost three-quarters larger than in the United Kingdom.

To buy a large house also means more work, time, and money to maintain it; to buy an oversized car means more effort and money to drive it.

This difference is made possible by the unique opportunity that our physical environment gives us to consume; that is, the population density in the US, 31 people per square kilometer, allows for the wide-spread construction and owner-ship of such "fully detached" family homes in a way that the population density in most of the rest of the industrialized world simply doesn't, which becomes apparent when we look at the population density of the Czech Republic (132 people per square kilometer), Germany (2322), or Japan (337/k2).

That such a large number of Americans can and do own a house leads to further consumption: having bought such a large house, there is the need to fill its considerable interior with all manner of furniture, refrigerators, freezers (often a second freezer is located in the basement, to allow the family to stock up on frozen foods), washers and dryers, and then in-dulge in the questionable practices that so many appliances can induce (as happens in the American southwest, where the sun can dry a pair of washed jeans within an hour if hung on an outside line, but most people own and use a dryer instead).

And, because parking is so ample in such a spacious coun-try, there is also the ability to own multiple cars, and in the suburbs more than one car per person in a household is by no means unusual. As a result, there are 765 registered cars per 1000 adults in the United States, while in the United Kingdom there are 426 per 1000, and in the Czech Republic 399 per 1000. And, as with "homeownership," we must also here clarify the exact nature of what we are describing, since by "car" we often, in the United States, are actually speaking of a truck; thus the most popular "car" in the US from 1991 to 2008 was the Ford F-150 pickup, which weighs 2200 kilos.

The Puritan work ethic was for a long time one of the ideological foundations of American society.

It however takes more than just available space to make possible the hyper-consumerism characteristic of the United States. It also takes the exuberance mentioned above—the de-sire—to do so. To buy a large house also means more work, time, and money to maintain it; to buy an oversized car means more effort and money to drive it. That so many have been persuaded to add these additional burdens unto themselves when there is no outstanding reason to do so illustrates the reality that consumerism possesses a singularly unique and dominant position culturally in the USA.

Limited Non-Consumer Options

This is not to suggest that it is, in general, difficult to consumerize a people. Indeed, Europe, Japan, and increasingly China already have full-blown consumer economies. However, to get these countries to consume at the level of the United States is quite another matter because there is more cultural resistance in them to consumerism. The United States doesn't have any remnants of the pre-industrial feudal culture or land use patterns that in Europe and Asia still tend to blunt the extremities of consumer capitalism. For example, the many forms of low-consumptive weekend outings that Czech people go on (and are typical of Europe in general) are not generally available in the United States: one can't, for example, take a passenger train to a small village because such trains long ago stopped running and, even if one could, or even if one drove their car there, it wouldn't be possible to follow a red, yellow, or green-marked "tourist" trail to some nearby point of interest as it is in Europe because the countryside in the United States has not only always been owned by private owners but, true to the principles of private property, fenced off by them as well.

The limited range of non-consumer options available to Americans, especially in the suburbs where the majority of the population lives, encourages the residents to take advantage of the one recreational opportunity that is readily available, which is to drive to a shopping mall or superstore and "shop till you drop."

Indeed, the main historical obstacle to consumerizing the United States was ideological, in the form of the celebrated Puritan work ethic. Derived from Calvinist doctrine and emphasizing hard work and thrift, the Puritan work ethic was for a long time one of the ideological foundations of American society. When, in the aftermath of World War II, industrial productivity had progressed to the stage where the economy required consumers to spend money and not thrifty workers to save money (toward capital accumulation), this ideological constraint was overcome with a massive propaganda campaign. Especially notable here was the effectiveness of the advertisements and programs in the new mass media of television extolling the various products and life-styles on offer.

The junkie characterization is especially apt when we consider that this level of consumption is something that we cannot sustain.

So, once the remaining physical obstacles were overcome— e.g. city public transit systems being bought out and arbitrarily eliminated or downsized by General Motors after World War II, the government spending trillions of dollars to build a highway system in the 1950s that destroyed inter-city train travel, huge incentives being given to returning soldiers after WWII to buy houses—there was little to stop Americans from going whole-hog into consumerism. So much so that, more than a mere addiction to consumerism (the populations of all the industrial economies, after all, seem to have at least a mild addiction to consumerism), the severity of America's addiction could be said to place us in the "junkie" category.

Indeed, since the last real resistance to consumer culture, the hippie, counter-cultural movement, was overcome in the course of the 1970s, this could be put in almost objective terms: the average house size in the United States, for example, increased from 1,750 square feet in 1978 to 2,479 in

2007; the best-selling car went from being the Ford Escort (1000 kilograms) in the early 1980s to the already mentioned Ford F-150 pickup (2200 kilograms) by the beginning of the 1990s; and even, on a personal and physical level, the prevalence of obesity among adults aged 20–74 years increased from 15.0% (in a 1976–1980 survey) to 34.6% (in a 2005–2006 survey). The junkie characterization is especially apt when we consider that this level of consumption is something that we cannot sustain. The chronic, huge, and unsustainable trade deficits, averaging around $700 billion a year over the past five years is proof enough of this, without even needing to delve into the longer-term energy and environmental unsustainability of it.

Creating Consumer Needs

Indeed, some world leaders, taking note of this, have started to play the role of social worker for our benefit, chiding us for our behavior and suggesting solutions. This would include the Chinese Premier Wen Jiabao. At a recent meeting on climate change, Wen stated that rich nations should alter their lifestyles—their "unsustainable way of life"—to help tackle global warming, and in an interview with *Business Week* magazine he blamed the world economic turmoil on the "inappropriate macroeconomic policies of some economies," meaning, especially, the United States, with its acceptance of "prolonged low savings and high consumption."

Many of the consumer-related aspects of the American economy . . . are not a sustainable model of economic development, much less a desirable one.

But there is something hypocritical in this, rather as though the drug dealer were chastising his best customer for her addiction while, at the same time, extending credit to her so she can buy more drugs. Indeed, this metaphor holds especially true for China, as almost the whole of China's much vaunted trade surplus with the world consists of their trade surplus with the United States (in 2008 China had a $309 billion trade surplus with the world, of which the USA accounted for $268 billion), while they are also our largest creditor nation (holding over $1 trillion of US debt). But China is by no means our only pusher, for we also supply an even larger proportion of Japan's overall trade surplus (Japan had an $80 billion trade surplus in 2008, of which the USA accounted for $74 billion), and it is our second largest creditor nation, holding $725 billion of our debt.

But perhaps addict and pusher aren't the right terms here. Perhaps all of us—as in the whole of the industrialized world—are instead caught up in a kind of shared delusion, or even codependency, in which we all pretend that capitalism still operates according to its classical principle that a need leads to a demand which leads to a product being produced. Or, as the French economist and philosopher Andre Gorz wrote in *Paths to Paradise: On the Liberation from Work*, "unlike earlier economic development, advanced capitalism is no longer propelled by a spontaneous dynamic of demand, reliant on what Marxists have always called 'basic needs:' those whose non-satisfaction is synonymous with destitution." Instead, with the most basic needs of its own populations having been met, it has been faced with the need to create a "subject for the object," of a demand for the supply. "From the mid-1950s onwards," Gorz continues, "the centers of capitalism were faced with the necessity to produce consumers for their commodities, needs to match the most profitable products. Following its spontaneous, capitalist dynamic, production had ceased to correspond to preexisting needs: in as much as such needs persisted (notably in housing, sanitation and public health) their satisfaction was not profitable, or not sufficiently so, for capital. And, conversely, the most profitable products did not match unsatisfied needs: these needs had to be created. Thus it was necessary to establish the material environment (chiefly through extensive urbanization) and social and cultural context which would foster them."

That the "material environment" of consumption of which Gorz writes has now apparently exhausted itself in the very nation where it could be developed to its fullest, and has probably been maximized to its physical and cultural limitations elsewhere, shows the need to rid ourselves of the traditional and no longer applicable measures of national economic well-being, such as the Gross Domestic Product (GDP). Especially when we consider that many of the consumer-related aspects of the American economy—huge trade deficits, high levels of consumer debt, the consumption of vast amounts of energy, cultural and social degeneration, environmental degradation—are not a sustainable model of economic development, much less a desirable one.

Organizations to Contact

The editors have compiled the following list of organizations concerned with the issues debated in this book. The descriptions are derived from materials provided by the organizations. All have publications or information available for interested readers. The list was compiled on the date of publication of the present volume; names, addresses, phone and fax numbers, and e-mail and Internet addresses may change. Be aware that many organizations take several weeks or longer to respond to inquiries, so allow as much time as possible.

American Enterprise Institute (AEI)
1150 Seventeenth St. NW, Washington, DC   20036
(202) 862-5800 • fax: (202) 862-7177
website: www.aei.org

The American Enterprise Institute (AEI) is a conservative think tank founded in 1943 to defend the principles and improve the institutions of American freedom and democratic capitalism. AEI promotes limited government, private enterprise, individual liberty and responsibility, vigilant and effective defense and foreign policies, political accountability, and open debate. Economic policy is one of AEI's research areas and its website is a source of many books and publications relating to the US economy. Recent articles include, for example, "Recession Blues" and "What Is Fiscally—and Politically—Sustainable?"

Brookings Institution
1775 Massachusetts Ave. NW, Washington, DC   20036
(202) 797-6000
website: www.brookings.edu

The Brookings Institution is a nonprofit public policy organization whose mission is to conduct high-quality, independent research and provide innovative, practical recommendations that advance three broad goals: strengthening American democracy; fostering the economic and social welfare, security, and opportunity of all Americans; and securing a more open, safe, prosperous, and cooperative international system. The group's website contains a section on the economy, where numerous publications on the current recession can be found. Two recent examples include "The U.S. Financial and Economic Crisis: Where Does It Stand and Where Do We Go From Here?" and "Financial Globalization and Economic Policies."

Cato Institute

1000 Massachusetts Ave. NW, Washington, DC   20001-5403
(202) 842-0200 • fax: (202) 842-3490
website: www.cato.org

The Cato Institute is a nonprofit public policy research foundation known for its libertarian viewpoints. The foundation's mission is to increase the understanding of public policies based on the principles of limited government, free markets, individual liberty, and peace. The group's website provides an extensive list of publications dealing with various public policy issues, including economic matters. Cato also publishes papers in the *Cato Journal* three times per year, the quarterly magazine *Regulation*, and a bimonthly newsletter, *Cato Policy Report*. Recent publications include "The Limits of Monetary Policy" and "Monetary Policy and Financial Regulation."

The Center for Global Development (CGD)

1800 Massachusetts Ave. NW, Third Floor
Washington, DC   20036
(202) 416-4000 • fax: (202) 416-4050
website: www.cgdev.org

The Center for Global Development (CGD) is an independent, nonprofit policy research organization dedicated to reducing global poverty and inequality and to making globalization work for the poor. The Center conducts research and actively engages policymakers and the public to influence the policies of the United States, other rich countries, and financial institutions such as the World Bank, the International Monetary Fund (IMF), and the World Trade Organization (WTO) to improve the economic and social development prospects in poor countries. CGD's website contains a list of publications which includes articles such as "How the Economic Crisis Is Hurting Africa—And What to Do About It" and "Blunt Instruments: On Establishing the Causes of Economic Growth."

Center for the Study of Income and Productivity (CSIP)

Federal Reserve Bank of San Francisco, 101 Market St.
Mail Stop 1130, San Francisco, CA   04105
(415) 974-3198
website: www.frbsf.org/csip

The Center for the Study of Income and Productivity (CSIP), organized under the Federal Reserve Bank of San Francisco's Economic Research Department, seeks to promote a better understanding of innovation and productivity and their links to the performance of national and regional economies in the United States. CSIP's core activity is research, but it also serves as a public resource, providing access to research, analysis, and selected data through the organization's website.

Economic Policy Institute (EPI)

1333 H St. NW, Suite 300, East Tower
Washington, DC   20005-4707
(202) 775-8810 • fax: (202) 775-0819
e-mail: researchdept@epi.org
website: www.epi.org

The Economic Policy Institute (EPI) is a nonprofit think tank created in 1986 to broaden the discussion about economic policy to include the interests of low- and middle-income workers. The group conducts research on the status of American workers and publishes a report called "State of Working America" every two years. The EPI website provides a list of publications, many of which concern US economic matters. Examples of publications include "Worst Downturn Since the Great Depression" and "Too Big to Fail . . . and Getting Bigger."

Federal Reserve System

20th St. and Constitution Ave. NW, Washington, DC   20551
website: www.federalreserve.gov

The Federal Reserve System, also known as the Fed, was created by Congress in 1913 to be the nation's central bank. It is made up of a seven-member Board of Governors, a twelve-member Federal Open Market Committee, twelve regional member banks located throughout the United States, and staff economists. The Federal Reserve's function is to control inflation without triggering a recession. In addition, the Fed supervises the nation's banking system to protect consumers, maintains the stability of the financial markets to prevent potential crises, and acts as the central bank for other banks, the US government, and foreign banks. The Fed's website is a source of economic research and data and consumer financial information.

The Heritage Foundation

214 Massachusetts Ave. NE, Washington, DC   20002-4999
(202) 546-4400 • fax: (202) 546-8328
website: www.heritage.org

The Heritage Foundation is a conservative public policy research institute founded in 1973 whose mission is to formulate and promote conservative public policies based on the principles of free enterprise, limited government, individual freedom, traditional American values, and a strong national defense. The economy is one of the institute's primary concerns and its website is a source of economic publications such as "Republicans' Financial Regulatory Reform Plan a Good Start" and "Government Intervention: A Threat to Economic Recovery."

National Bureau of Economic Research (NBER)
1050 Massachusetts Ave., Cambridge
Massachusetts   02138-5398
(617) 868-3900 • fax: (617) 868-2742
website: www.nber.org

Founded in 1920, the National Bureau of Economic Research (NBER) is a private, nonprofit, nonpartisan research organization that undertakes and supports unbiased economic research among public policymakers, business professionals, and the academic community. A search of the NBER website produces numerous working papers and other information on various economic issues, including the 2007–09 recession. Examples of recent publications include "The Credit Rating Crisis" and "Inflation and the Stock Market: Understanding the 'Fed Model.'"

US Department of the Treasury
1500 Pennsylvania Ave. NW, Washington, DC   20220
(202) 622-2000 • fax: (202) 622-6415
website: www.ustreas.gov

The US Department of the Treasury is the executive agency responsible for promoting economic prosperity and ensuring the financial security of the United States. The department is responsible for a wide range of activities, such as advising the President on economic and financial issues, encouraging sustainable economic growth, and fostering improved governance in financial institutions. The Treasury Department's website is a source of news and other information about the US economy, including various government initiatives such as the Emergency Economic Stabilization Act—Troubled Asset Relief Program (TARP) and other actions being taken to combat economic recession in the United States.

Bibliography

Books

Daron Acemoglu and James Robinson
Why Nations Fail: The Origins of Power, Prosperity, and Poverty. New York: Crown Business, 2012.

Richard Duncan
The New Depression: The Breakdown of the Paper Money Economy. Hoboken, NJ: Wiley, 2012.

Simon Johnson and James Kwak
13 Bankers: The Wall Street Takeover and the Next Financial Meltdown. New York: Vintage, 2011.

Simon Johnson and James Kwak
White House Burning: The Founding Fathers, Our National Debt, and Why It Matters to You. New York: Pantheon, 2012.

Paul Krugman
End This Depression Now! New York: W.W. Norton, 2012.

Chris Martenson
The Crash Course: The Unsustainable Future of Our Economy, Energy, and Environment. Hoboken, NJ: Wiley, 2011.

Bethany McLean and Joe Nocera
All the Devils Are Here: The Hidden History of the Financial Crisis. New York: Portfolio Trade, 2011.

Carmen M. Reinhart and Kenneth Rogoff
This Time Is Different: Eight Centuries of Financial Folly. Princeton, NJ: Princeton University, 2009.

James Rickards — *Currency Wars: The Making of the Next Global Crisis.* New York: Portfolio, 2011.

Nouriel Roubini — *Crisis Economics.* New York: Allen Lane, 2010.

Nouriel Roubini and Stephen Mihm — *Crisis Economics: A Crash Course in the Future of Finance.* New York: Penguin, 2011.

Peter D. Schiff — *How the Economy Grows and Why It Crashes.* Hoboken, NJ: Wiley, 2010.

Peter D. Schiff — *The Real Crash: America's Coming Bankruptcy—How to Save Yourself and Your Country.* New York: St. Martin's, 2012.

Robert J. Shiller — *Finance and the Good Society.* Princeton, NJ: Princeton University, 2012.

Peter J. Tanous and Jeff Cox — *Debt, Deficits, and the Demise of the American Economy.* Hoboken, NJ: Wiley, 2011.

Periodicals and Internet Sources

Zaheer Abbasi — "Economy Facing Serious Challenges, US Told," *Business Recorder*, April 5, 2012.

Leonie Barrie — "US Retail Sales Warmed by Spring Sunshine in March," Just-Style.com, April 10, 2012. www.just-style.com.

Grant Bowers   "Sustainable Expansion in the US Economy," *Investment Advisor*, March 26, 2012.

Business Daily Update   "How Will 'Two Sessions' Set Tune for China's Economy?" March 5, 2012.

Philip Coggan   "The Patient Is Still in Recovery," *Investment Adviser*, April 9, 2012.

Julie Crawshaw   "Gary Shilling: 2012 Recession Still Coming," *Newsmax*, April 4, 2012.

Credit Union Journal   "CUs, Banks Stand to Lose if USPS Suffers Big Cuts, Hikes Postage Rates," April 16, 2012.

Financial Express   "Column: The American Recovery," March 26, 2012.

Bradley Gerrard   "Morning Papers: US Economy Contrasts with Eurozone," *Investment Adviser*, April 9, 2012.

Jill Goldsmith   "Rosy Forecast for TV's Selling Season," *Daily Variety*, March 14, 2012.

Forrest Jones   "Expert: Consumer Confidence to Fall This Summer," *Newsmax*, March 6, 2012.

Forrest Jones   "Gallup: Half See Country Stuck in Recession or Depression," *Newsmax*, March 7, 2012.

Aaron G. Lehmer and Kristen Schwind — "The Resilient Future for the 99%," *Earth Island Journal*, Winter 2012.

Elaine Misonzhnik — "Restaurant Chains Poised for Growth in 2012," *Retail Traffic*, March 22, 2012.

Russell Parera — "Provide Stimulus in Key Sectors," *Financial Express*, March 8, 2012.

James Surowiecki — "Great Expectations?" *New Yorker*, March 19, 2012.

Kevin Wack — "Banks Have Big Stake in Battle Over Postal Reform," *American Banker*, April 10, 2012.

Index

CPSIA information can be obtained
at www.ICGtesting.com
Printed in the USA
FFOW040644271112
341FF

9 780737 762143